MIND-BLOWING
MAGIC TRICKS
FOR EVERYONE

MIND-BLOWING
MAGIC TRICKS
FOR EVERYONE

50 STEP-BY-STEP CARD, COIN, AND MENTALISM TRICKS THAT ANYONE CAN DO

OSCAR OWEN
Viral YouTube Magician

Skyhorse Publishing

Skyhorse Publishing books may be purchased in bulk at special discounts for sales promotion, corporate gifts, fund-raising, or educational purposes. Special editions can also be created to specifications. For details, contact the Special Sales Department, Skyhorse Publishing, 307 West 36th Street, 11th Floor, New York, NY 10018 or info@skyhorsepublishing.com.

Skyhorse® and Skyhorse Publishing® are registered trademarks of Skyhorse Publishing, Inc.®, a Delaware corporation.

Visit our website at www.skyhorsepublishing.com.

10 9 8 7 6 5 4 3

Library of Congress Cataloging-in-Publication Data is available on file

Cover design by Kai Texel
Cover photograph by Oscar Owen

Print ISBN: 978-1-5107-6330-2
E-Book ISBN: 978-1-5107-6577-1

Printed in China

To Mum and Dad, for being magical inspirations in my life.

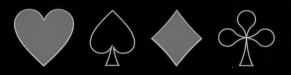

The More You Look, the Less You See.

CONTENTS

What if you could look at someone directly in the eye and know exactly what they were thinking? What if you could crack an apple open with your bare hands? What if you could guess the password to anyone's phone?

This book is going to give you a masterclass in mind-blowing magic and reveal the methods behind some of the greatest illusions ever created. Packed inside these pages are more than fifty foolproof tricks that I have handpicked from over a decade of performing magic. All of these tricks are easy to do, require no previous experience, and always get crazy reactions.

I've split this book into seven different sections. In the first section, I'll explain exactly how you should practice your magic. Knowing the right way to practice is essential because it allows you to learn tricks faster and perform them more confidently.

After that, we will look at my favorite card tricks. I will teach you the exact effects that have taken me around the world to perform at some of the most exclusive events and festivals on the planet. Next, I reveal eight incredible coin tricks that are perfect for doing at a party, bar, gathering, or any situation where you've got some coins.

The third section then delves into the realm of mentalism. Here you will learn how to read the mind of your spectator, predict the future, and even put thoughts into someone's head.

Section four looks at magic with everyday objects. This includes tearing up and restoring napkins, making cups penetrate through a solid table, as well as vanishing pens into thin air.

Next, I teach you my favorite bets. These are perfect to do when you are out with friends having a drink and want to show them something that shouldn't be possible (such as balancing a coin on the edge of a banknote!) The final section then gives you tips on how to perform your magic: explaining what to say when doing the trick, what to wear, and how to speak clearly and confidently.

You'll notice that many of the step-by-step images in this book have QR codes printed on the top left-hand corner. If you take your phone, open up the camera app and scan the QR code, you'll be taken to a performance of the trick. These performances will help you understand and visualize what the effect actually looks like before you try to learn it.

Ultimately, you can consider this book to be a little "magic bible" and the definitive guide to being the most interesting person in the room. The pages that follow will reveal the highly-guarded secrets behind some of magic's most powerful tricks. So go and grab a deck of cards, open your mind, and get ready to dive head-first into this colorful, deceptive and mysterious ancient art form that we call "magic."

About Your Instructor

Oscar Owen is an award-winning close-up magician and YouTuber. Magic has taken him all over the world to astonish large audiences and celebrity guests at some of the most high-end red-carpet events and festivals on the planet. Since 2016 he has been teaching magic on YouTube; amassing hundreds of thousands of subscribers and millions of views from over 120 countries. Internationally known for easy-to-follow tutorials that reveal mind-blowing magic tricks, Oscar has brought all his passion and knowledge for teaching magic into this book. By following his simple instructions laid out on the pages ahead, you will learn how to astonish anyone you meet with nothing more than a deck of cards or random objects lying around the house.

YouTube: https://www.youtube.com/oscarowen

Instagram: https://www.instagram.com/0scar/

HOW TO PRACTICE

I've written this book with the average person in mind by making sure that the tricks inside take minutes (not weeks) to master. This is so that you can get out there and start performing right away. All of these effects are either self-working or require minimal sleight of hand, meaning that anyone can do them regardless of previous experience and confidence levels. Nevertheless, you still need to put in practice so that you can perform these effects with conviction. Below I have outlined a practical three-step approach that will help you prepare, practice, and perform each trick.

Step 1: Practice the sleights

Sleights tend to be the hardest part of any trick and so you should begin by practicing them in isolation. Sit in front of a mirror and repeat the sleight over and over again—not until you get it right, but until you cannot get it wrong. Once you have mastered it, the trick will be significantly easier to perform.

Step 2: Practice the trick

Now you want to practice the entire trick from start to finish and become familiar with its mechanics, such as when to shuffle, when to perform the sleight, when to reveal their card, etc. Once the structure of the trick has become second nature, your presentation will be much more coherent, meaning the entire effect can flow naturally.

Step 3: Practice your presentation

Finally, you want to rehearse what you are going to say during your performance. Think of a story that complements the trick, and then practice saying it out loud. What you say is just as important as what you do! Your patter should help captivate your audience by building suspense and adding comedic value. See page 137 for some tips on how to craft an effective presentation. Make sure you scan the QR codes with your phone to see an example performance.

> "The tricks themselves are often very simple
> and the art of the conjurer lies in dressing
> them up so that they appear to be miraculous."
> —WILFRID JONSON, 1950

CARD TRICKS

Everybody is familiar with card magic regardless of their age, gender, or background. As such, every magician should know some strong card effects that they can perform at a moment's notice. We are therefore going to begin by learning ten powerful card tricks that you can do anytime, anywhere, and in any place. Some of these tricks can be done entirely impromptu while others require you to set up the cards in advance secretly. Either way, I must warn you: no one will want to play cards with you after you have learned these tricks.

FOUNDATIONAL CARD MOVES

Even though magicians have created thousands of card moves, there are only a handful that they regularly use. Some of the tricks taught in this book require no sleight of hand whatsoever, while others will need you to know how to pull off a "card force" and a "card control."

A card force gives the impression that the spectator randomly selected a card when, in reality, the magician made him pick it. A card control allows you to secretly move the spectator's selection to the top of the deck without them knowing.

I'm going to teach you a few different ways to perform both of these foundational card moves. You don't need to learn them all, but make sure you master at least one card force and one card control. Doing so will instantly unlock your ability to perform hundreds of incredibly powerful magic tricks that you can use to entertain and bewilder your spectators.

FORCING A CARD

Here are three simple yet deceptive ways to force a card.

METHOD 1:
CRISS-CROSS FORCE (BEGINNER)

▶ Watch Video

1. You need to know what the top card in the deck is since that is the card that you will be forcing onto your spectator. In this case it is the Ace of Spades. Once you know the top card, place the deck on the table.

3. Pick up what was the bottom packet, rotate it 90 degrees, and lay it across the top packet. Tell your spectator that you are marking where they cut the deck.

2. Ask the spectator to cut the cards in half so that there are two packets on the table. You need to remember which packet was originally on top.

4. Misdirect the spectators from the playing cards for around 10 seconds. You can do this by asking them questions such as "Did you feel like I influenced where you cut the cards?" This misdirection causes the spectator to forget which packet they cut to. Now lift off the top packet and point to the pile that is still on the table. Tell your spectator to turn over the top card on this pile and remember it.

5 They will think it is the card that they cut to, but it is, of course, the forced card.

▶ Watch Video

1 Make sure the card that you want to force is on the top of the deck. In this example, we will be forcing the Ace of Hearts.

2 Now hold the deck in your non-dominant hand. Place your thumb along one edge of the cards and your middle, ring, and pinkie finger along the opposite edge as shown.

3 Then curl your index finger under the deck and use your thumb to riffle down the cards. As you riffle down the cards, ask your spectator to say "Stop" whenever they like.

4 Come in with your dominant hand and lift up the top packet from where your spectator told you to stop. However, as you do this, make sure your middle, ring, and pinkie finger maintain pressure on the top card.

5 This will cause the top card to slide onto the bottom packet. You can then present your spectator with the card they think they stopped at. They will not be aware that they are holding your forced card.

METHOD 3: HINDU FORCE (ADVANCED)

▶ Watch Video

1 Place the card that you want to force on the bottom of the deck. We will be forcing the spectator to select the Ace of Hearts in this example.

2 Hold the deck high up in the fingertips of your non-dominant hand. You want your thumb along the edge closest to you, your index finger on the top edge, and your middle, ring, and pinkie fingers contacting the side of the deck opposite your thumb.

3 Remove the bottom three-quarters of the deck using your thumb and middle finger on your dominant hand. Take these cards and then move them away from your non-dominant hand.

4 Allow the remaining cards in your non-dominant hand to fall into your palm.

5 Now move your dominant hand forward again until it is directly over the cards that just fell into your palm. Use the tips of your non-dominant thumb and middle finger to lift off a small packet of cards from the top of the pile in your dominant hand. Let these cards slide off the deck and fall on top of the cards that are already in your non-dominant hand.

6 Repeat this motion over and over again. The cards will peel off in small chunks and land in your non-dominant hand.

The Hindu Force works by creating the illusion that you are shuffling all the cards when in reality the bottom card of the packet held in your dominant hand never actually changes.

7 As you do so, ask your spectator to call out "Stop" whenever they like. When you are instructed to stop, lift up the packet in your dominant hand and show them the bottom card. This will be the forced card.

CONTROLLING A CARD

Here are two easy ways to control a card to the top of the deck.

METHOD 1:
THE BLUFF CONTROL (BEGINNER)

Watch Video

1 Have your spectator choose a card.

2 While they are looking at their card, you have all the misdirection in the world to secretly turn over the bottom card in the deck. I have turned over the Jack of Clubs in this example.

3 Cut the cards in half and place the top packet onto the table. Keep the other packet (with the facedown card) in your hand.

4 Ask your spectator to return their card on top of the pile that is situated on the table.

! Now place the packet of cards that is in your hand on top of the table pile.

6 Pick up the cards and begin to spread through them. Explain to your spectator that you have no idea where their card is. At some point, you will come across the face-up card. Act surprised and say, "Oh, this shouldn't be face up!"

Here is the clever part. The card *under* the face-up card is the spectator's selection. So, break the deck into two piles from the face-up card. Make sure the spectator's selection is at the top of one of the two piles.

8 Now bring the packet that has the spectator's selection to the top of the deck. This will simultaneously move the face-up card to the bottom of the deck. Flip over the face-up card so it is the right way around. Then casually continue with the trick. Your spectator's selection will now be on top of the deck!

PRO TIP:

If you find yourself in a situation where you don't feel confident turning the bottom card over in front of your spectators (Step 2) then simply begin the control with the bottom card already turned over as seen in the performance video!

METHOD 2:
THE CUT CONTROL (INTERMEDIATE)

Watch Video

THE SPECTATOR'S CARD

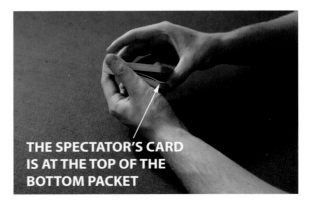

THE SPECTATOR'S CARD IS AT THE TOP OF THE BOTTOM PACKET

1 Have the spectator choose any card they like. Then take their card in your dominant hand and explain that you are going to lose it somewhere into the deck. Push their card into the back of the deck (about halfway down) until only an inch of it is sticking out.

2 At this point, press down on their card with your thumb while you push it forward. You will notice that this causes the deck to break into two packets. The top card on the bottom packet will be the spectator's selection.

PINKIE BREAK

3 Now place the little finger of your non-dominant hand into the gap you just created. This means that your pinkie finger is directly on the spectator's card. This is called a pinkie break.

4 For clarification, there should now be two packets in your hand. At the top of the bottom packet is the spectator's card and your pinkie finger is separating both packets. Now, simply take half of the top packet and place it onto the table. Then take the second half of the top packet and put that onto the table, too. Finally, place the bottom packet onto the table.

5 The spectator's card will have been controlled to the top.

PRO TIP:

When performing the cut control, remember to not lose sight of the bigger picture. From the spectator's perspective, you are not controlling anything! Therefore don't make a big deal out of cutting the cards. Rather, just causally cut them as if nothing is going on—your spectator will be none the wiser that you know exactly where their card is.

KEEP A POKER FACE OR I'LL GUESS YOUR CARD!

EFFECT:

The spectator chooses a card, remembers it, and then returns it into the deck. The spectator then cuts the cards as many times as they want so neither they nor the magician knows where the card is. The magician then deals the cards face up onto the table and tells the spectator to keep a poker face and to give nothing away. Nevertheless, despite the spectator's best efforts, the magician impossibly stops dealing at the spectator's card!

PREPARATION:

You will need a deck of cards.

PERFORMANCE:

1 Begin by letting the spectator shuffle the cards up. Then take the cards back and let them freely choose one.

2 While they are looking at their selection, secretly get a glimpse at the bottom card in the deck. For example, in this case, it is the Six of Hearts. This will be our Key Card.

MAGICIAN DEALS
CARDS INTO A PILE

THE SPECTATOR'S
SELECTION

From here, deal small piles of cards onto the table from the top of the deck. Tell your spectator that they can place their card on top of the table pile whenever they like.

You know that the card after the Key Card will be the spectator's selection!

4 When they put their card down, place the cards that are in your hand on top. This is a very deceptive way to give the impression that the spectator randomly returned their card into the deck. However, your Key Card (that you remembered earlier) is now on top of their selection.

From here, let the spectator cut the cards as many times as they like. (The Key Card will always remain on top of the selection. **This is because cutting the cards does not change the order of the deck, it simply changes the position of the top and bottom card.**) When they are happy, take the deck back and start to deal cards face up onto the table. Keep dealing until you see the Key Card (which is the Six of Hearts in this case).

PRO TIPS:

- The secret behind this effect is straightforward, meaning you can really focus on how you *present* the trick. When performing, emphasize the fact that you are going to read the spectator's body language. Tell them to keep a poker face and not to give anything away. People will genuinely believe that you are studying their micro-movements to determine what their card is!

- The only time this trick becomes challenging is if the spectator cuts directly in between your Key Card and their selection. This would result in their card on the top of the deck and the Key Card on the bottom of the deck. However, this is really easy to spot. Once the spectator has finished cutting the cards, simply turn the deck over casually and glance at the bottom card. If it happens to be your Key Card, then give the deck one final cut and everything will be back to normal!

THE LAZY MAN'S CARD TRICK

EFFECT:

The magician explains that he is going to demonstrate "card tracking." This is where he is able to tell exactly where the spectator's card is in the deck without even touching it! The spectator proceeds to choose any card they like. They then lose it back into the pack and cut it multiple times. Without even touching the deck, the magician can tell exactly how many cards from the top the spectator's card is.

PREPARATION:

A   Before you begin, pull out the Ace of Spades through the Ten of Spades and place them on the bottom of the deck in order. Make sure the ace is on the very bottom.

PERFORMANCE:

1   Ask someone to pick a card, look at it, and remember it. You want to make sure that they only do not choose one of the ten cards that you just stacked at the bottom of the deck. To be sure of this, you can either force them the top card using the "Slip Cut Force" taught on page 8 or spread out the cards in your hand but only display the top third of the deck.

Now hold the deck in your hand and start to deal small piles down onto the table.

3 Let the spectator put their card back onto the table pile whenever they like. This is a free choice. Then place the rest of the cards on top.

This will position the ten cards that you pulled out earlier on top of the spectator's card. Now turn the deck over so that it is face up. Ask your spectator to cut the cards in half (so that there are two piles) and then to complete the cut (so that there is one pile again). This will mix up the cards, making it seem impossible for you to track their selection!

5, 6 Now here is the where the magic happens. What you are trying to do is get the spectator to cut somewhere into the ten-card stack that you created earlier. If they do cut somewhere into this stack, then continue onto the next step. If they do not, make them cut the deck again and again until they do!

7 If they cut to the Six of Spades, then turn the deck over and their card will be sixth from the top. Likewise, if they cut to the Eight of Spades, then their card will be eight from the top. For the reveal, concentrate very hard and act as if you are doing some complex calculations that will allow you to track their card. Suddenly snap your fingers and reveal how many cards from the top their selection is!

PRO TIP:

The wonderful thing about this effect is that the spectator is the one who handles the deck, which makes it seem impossible for you to be able to track their selection. As such, you should emphasize this point by saying "To make this as fair as possible, I don't want to touch the cards at all. Please can you cut the cards for me?" I often also make the spectator cut the cards at least four times, to make it seem even more impossible that I am able to track their selection.

A CRAZY SELF-WORKING PREDICTION

EFFECT:

The spectator eliminates some red cards and some black cards from the deck. The magician correctly guesses how many red and black cards the spectator eliminates *before* the trick even begins!

PERFORMANCE:

1 Tell your spectator to give the deck a shuffle. They won't be aware that it is already missing four black cards. Once they are happy, instruct them to deal cards off the top of the deck two at a time. If both cards they deal are red, then put them in one pile. If both cards are black, put them in a separate pile, and if one card is red and one card is black then put them in yet another pile. The spectator will go through the cards, dealing two at a time. They will separate them into a red, black, and mixed pile as instructed.

PREPARATION:

A Write down a prediction on a folded piece of paper that says, "There will be four more red cards than black cards." You now need to get a deck of cards that is complete (meaning it has fifty-two cards excluding jokers). Remove 4 black cards from the deck (you can just leave them in the box). Now you're ready to begin.

2 The spectator can shuffle and mix up the cards as much as they like! The only rule is they need to turn the cards over two at a time. Once this is done, remove the mixed pile since it is not needed. They will now be left with the red and black pile.

3 Open your prediction that says, "There will be four more red cards than black cards." Tell your spectator to count out the number of cards in both piles. To their amazement, your prediction will be correct.

PRO TIP:

This is one of those awesome mathematical tricks that always works. I present this trick by saying the following. "Last night I had a strange dream that you [the spectator] eliminated a certain number of black cards and red cards from this deck [point to the cards]. I woke up from my dream and wrote down a prediction. Let's see if it was correct."

DO AS I DO

EFFECT:

The magician and spectator each shuffle their own deck of cards. They then both select any card they like from their shuffled decks and both cards perfectly match. This is easily one of the greatest card tricks ever created and an effect that I often use in my professional shows.

PREPARATION:

You will need two decks of cards, ideally different colors.

PERFORMANCE:

1 Give one deck to your spectator and keep the other for yourself. Shuffle up your cards in any way that you please. Instruct the spectator to do exactly the same.

THE MAGICIAN REMEMBERS THE BOTTOM CARD

2 Once you are both satisfied that everything is thoroughly mixed, secretly look at and remember the bottom card in your deck. This will be your Key Card.

THE SPECTATOR AND MAGICIAN HAVE SWAPPED DECKS

3 Now switch decks with your spectator and tell them to copy your moves exactly.

THE SPECTATOR & MAGICIAN CUT THE CARDS IN HALF

THEY REMEMBER THE NEXT CARD DOWN

4 Hold the cards in your right hand and cut around half of them off. Place this half onto the table. Tell your spectator to do the same.

5 Now turn over the next card from the pile in your hand and remember it. Then place this card on the pile on the table. Instruct your spectator to do the same.

THE DECKS ARE SWAPPED AGAIN

THE SPECTATOR'S CARD IS IN THIS PILE AND IS RIGHT NEXT TO THE KEY CARD YOU REMEMBERED EARLIER

6 Finally, put the rest of the deck on top of the pile on the table. Again, instruct your spectator to also do this. Because your spectator has followed your actions exactly, the card that they just cut to is next to the Key Card that you remembered earlier.

7 Swap decks again. For clarification, this is the situation you should now be in. You now have your original deck back. Somewhere inside this deck is the card that the spectator cut to, and directly next to that card is the Key Card that you remembered earlier! To further lose your selections in the deck, cut the cards two more times.

8 Now tell your spectator that you are both going to find the card that you cut to. Go through your deck and find the Key Card. The card after the Key Card will be the spectator's selection.

PRO TIP:

This trick is a classical masterpiece. It seems so unbelievably fair, yet you will have matching cards 100 percent of the time. At the end, make sure you dress up this improbability by mentioning that "We both randomly shuffled and cut the cards. We then even switched decks and chose any card that we liked! What are the chances that these two cards here match?"

9, 10 Take their selection and place it in the middle of the table and tell them to do the same. When you turn over the cards, they will impossibly match!

MID-AIR CARD CHANGE

EFFECT:

The magician shakes a card and it visually changes in mid-air. This is a fun, quick, and impressive trick that you can do with a borrowed deck at a moment's notice!

PREPARATION:

All you need is a deck of cards. Practicing this effect in front of a mirror will help you see what the color change looks like from the spectator's point of view.

PERFORMANCE:

1 Turn over the top card in the deck. Then use your thumb to riffle up the back of the cards. Keep riffling until you get a break under the top two cards.

2 Pick them both up with your dominant hand. Do this by placing your middle finger on the top left corner of the cards and your thumb on the bottom right corner as shown.

3 Use your thumb and middle finger to bend the cards slightly. Then take your index finger and make contact with their outermost edge.

4, 5, 6 Now pull your index finger towards your hand. This will flip over both cards so that the bottom one rotates to the top.

Finally, do that exact same move while shaking your arm. This is very important since the big action of shaking your arm hides the small action of flipping the cards over. This will create a deceptive illusion that the card visually changed in the air.

PRO TIP:

To turn this card change into a card trick, do the following. Ask your spectator to choose a card. Return it into the deck and control it to the top using the cut control. Now claim that you are going to find your spectators selection. Pull out any card from the deck (but not the top card) and say, "Was this it?" Of course, your spectator will say "No." Then place this card on top of the deck face up. Perform the shake change and magically transform the wrong card into your spectator's selection!

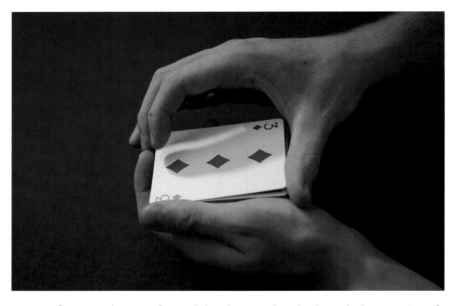

7 Once you have performed the change, place both cards down on top of the deck.

8 Since the bottom card will be the same orientation as the rest of the cards, you can secretly deposit it on top of the deck. From here, you can hand out the new card to be inspected.

CARD IN ORANGE

EFFECT:

This is a special effect that people will remember for years to come. The spectator selects a card. That card then disappears from the deck and reappears inside an orange! I often close my professional routine with this exact trick.

PRO TIP:

Remember that oranges are citrus fruits and so their acidic properties will start to eat away at the card. Therefore, I recommend that you perform this trick within 24 hours of preparing the orange. Any longer and the card will be almost unrecognizable when you reveal it!

PREPARATION:

A Before performing this trick, you will need to prepare the orange and the cards. The following props are required: two identical cards, an orange, a pencil, some glue, and some double-sided tape.

B To prepare for this trick, take one of the duplicate cards and roll it up into a tube.

C Then remove the calyx from the orange. Push the pencil deep into the orange so that there is enough space for the rolled-up card to fit inside.

D Place the card into this newly created hole.

E Then use some glue to stick the calyx back on top. This creates the illusion that the orange is completely normal when there is actually a card hidden inside it. Place the orange into the fruit bowl.

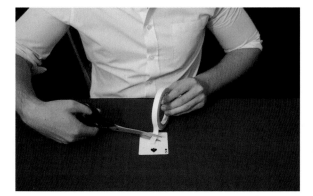

F Now take the other duplicate card and attach a square of double-sided tape to its face.

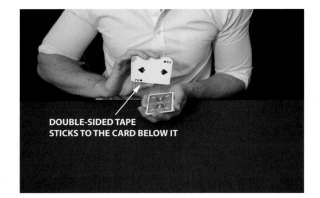

DOUBLE-SIDED TAPE
STICKS TO THE CARD BELOW IT

G Now place this card on the bottom of the deck and you are ready to begin.

PERFORMANCE:

1 The actual performance of this trick is quite simple. Using the "Hindu Force" (page 10), make your spectator choose the duplicate card on the bottom of the deck. Show it to them and then put it back on top of the pack. Because the card has double-sided tape on it, it will stick to the card below it. This means that when you spread through the deck, their card will have apparently disappeared.

PRO TIP:

To make the reveal in the orange even more impressive, say the following: "As you can see, your card has vanished from the deck! Do you know where it has gone? No? Well, it magically jumped into my top pocket!" At this point your spectators will exclaim something like, "No way, that's impossible!" Then dramatically open up your top pocket, only to show that there is actually nothing inside it. Make a joke saying "Well . . . I'm not actually that good!" Your spectators will not only find this funny; it also sets up a precedent that the card reveal in your top pocket would have been a miracle. This means that when you reveal that their card is in the orange (something that is far more impressive than the card being in your pocket), your spectator's minds will be even more blown!

2, 3, 4 Now point to the fruit bowl and pick out the orange. Slowly cut it open and reveal that the spectator's card has transported inside it!

BECOME A MASTER PICKPOCKET!

EFFECT:

The magician explains that he has spent several years studying how the best pickpockets in the world steal money. He wants to give the spectators a demonstration, but reassures them that he will use cards instead of real cash! The spectator freely chooses any card and returns it to the deck. All the cards are placed in the box and then the box goes into the magician's pocket. The magician then claims that in less than three seconds, he will reach into his pocket, open the box, riffle through the cards, find the spectator's card by feeling it, close the box and place the spectator's card on the table without looking—just how a pickpocket would take money out of a wallet! Of course, the spectator thinks this is impossible, but the magician actually does it.

PREPARATION:

All you need is a deck of cards and its box. A new deck of cards is preferable, but this will also work with an old deck too. And no, you will not need to spend ten years mastering this seemingly impossible stunt because, as you're about to find out, this trick is nearly self-working!

PERFORMANCE:

 Watch Video

1 Let the spectator choose any card they like.

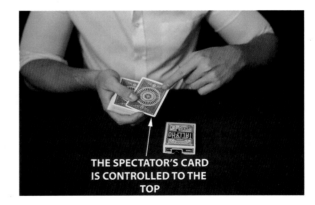

THE SPECTATOR'S CARD IS CONTROLLED TO THE TOP

2 Control the card the spectator chooses to the top of the deck using "The Cut Control" (page 14) or "The Bluff Control" (page 12).

THIS IS THE SPECTATOR'S SELECTION

3 Now put all of the cards inside the box. However, you want to make sure that the spectator's card is on the side where the flap enters the box as shown.

5, 6 This will allow you to place the flap of the box behind the spectator's card.

4 As you close the box, squeeze the sides near the opening together using your thumb and index finger. The cards will pop outwards.

7 Put all the cards in your pocket and as you do so, use your thumb to drag their selection upwards until it is around an inch out of the deck.

PRO TIP:

This is the most important part of the trick. Therefore, when practicing, isolate this move and do it over and over again until it becomes second nature!

8 At this point, your spectator thinks their card is somewhere in the pack when in reality it is sticking out of the box. From here, claim you are going to reach into your pocket, open the box, feel for their card, pull it out, close the box, and place their card on the table—all in less than three seconds without looking. Of course, you just need to reach into your pocket and take out the spectator's card that is already protruding from the deck.

PRO TIP:

If you want to turn this into a funny routine then I like to begin the trick by saying "So my father is in the 'steel' industry, so pickpocketing comes naturally to me." If the spectator has a nice watch on, you can then point it out and say something like "Wow that watch looks very nice—I wonder how much it would sell for online?" This always gets a nervous laugh and builds excitement. You can then say, "Look, I know you don't want me to actually take your money, so I'll use a deck of cards as an example instead." This provides a nice route into performing the trick.

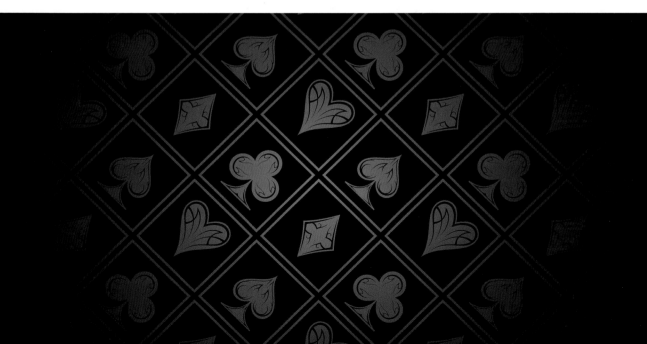

THE TRICK THAT FOOLED ALBERT EINSTEIN

EFFECT:

The spectator and magician both randomly cut off several cards from the deck. The magician then makes an impossible prediction about the cards they selected. This effect is so good, it even fooled Albert Einstein!

PRO TIP:

Begin this effect by saying to your spectator, "What I am about to show you is an old trick that was used to fool Albert Einstein. Watch me very carefully. . . ." This will immediately grab their attention and keep them captivated throughout the entire performance.

B Now place this stack of twenty-two cards on the bottom of the deck. If you hold the deck on its side, you will notice a small natural break created by the bend in the cards. This will be very important later on. Place the cards on the table.

PREPARATION:

A Before the trick begins, count off twenty-two cards. Pick up these cards and bend them using your thumb and fingers.

PERFORMANCE:

THE SPECTATOR'S PILE

1 Ask your spectator to cut off a small number of cards from the top of the deck. It is very important that you say "small" number of cards because you don't want your spectator to cut off more than twenty.

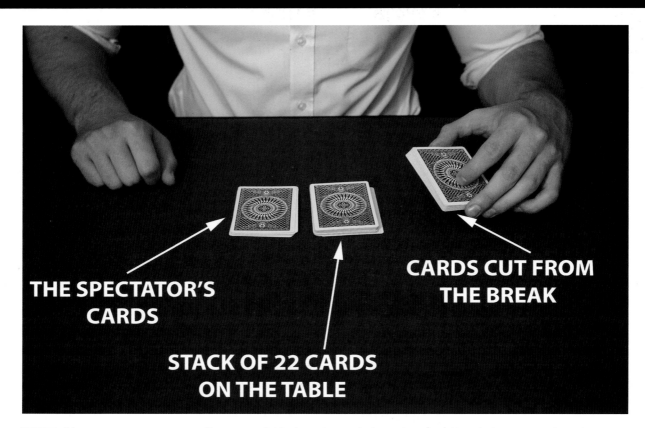

THE SPECTATOR'S CARDS

STACK OF 22 CARDS ON THE TABLE

CARDS CUT FROM THE BREAK

2 Now it is your turn to cut off some cards. Pick up the cards from the natural break that you made earlier. Move the cards in your hand to the side because they are not needed. You will now be left with the twenty-two cards that you secretly counted off beforehand which were on the bottom of the deck. While performing the move described above, say to your spectator "I am also going to cut some cards, but this time from the bottom of the pile to make things even more random!" Little do they know that the cards left on the table are actually your stack.

3 From here the trick is self-working! Pick up both piles and pretend to weigh them. Then say the following prediction: "From feeling the weight of both piles, I can tell you the difference between the number of cards we have both just randomly cut off the deck. My prediction is this: I have as many cards as you have, plus two extra cards and enough left over to bring your total number of cards up to twenty."

SPECTATOR'S 10
CARDS

THE MAGICIAN DEALS
DOWN 10 CARDS FROM
HIS PILE

THE MAGICIAN ADDS
TWO EXTRA CARDS TO HIS PILE

4 Regardless of how many cards the spectator chooses (so long as it is less than twenty), your prediction will always be correct. Tell the spectator to count out how many cards they have onto the table. Then repeat the prediction in stages. In this example, the magician says, "I have as many cards as you have." The spectator has ten cards, so the magician deals ten cards down from his pile.

5 "Plus two extra cards" and the magician adds two more cards to his pile.

THE REST OF THE CARDS ARE ADDED TO BRING
THE SPECTATOR'S PILE UP TO TWENTY

6 "And enough left over to bring your total to twenty" and the magician adds the rest of his cards to the spectator's pile and brings their total up to twenty. Regardless of how many cards the spectator cut off the deck, the remaining cards in your hand will always bring their total up to twenty!

DON'T PICK THE ODD CARD!

EFFECT:

The magician lets the spectator select one of eight face-up cards. The spectator turns over their freely selected card and it is blue. The magician turns over all the other cards and they are all red. This is a fun easy trick that you can learn in a matter of minutes.

PREPARATION:

A You will need two separate decks: one blue and one red. Take four blue-backed cards and four-red backed cards. Make sure that they have different faces.

B Now place the red and blue cards in an alternating order so that they go red-blue-red-blue, etc.

PRO TIP:

This is what is known as a "packet trick" since it only uses a few cards. I like to set up the cards in advance and then place them into an envelope so that I can always do this trick at a moment's notice without preparing it in front of the spectator.

PERFORMANCE:

1 Display all eight cards face up to your spectator. It is very important that they do not see the back of these cards. Now let the spectator point to any card that they like. This is a genuinely free choice so emphasize the fact that they can change their mind. In this example, the spectator has pointed to the Nine of Hearts.

2 Once they have pointed to a card, you need to bring it to the top of the pile. Take all the cards above the spectator's selection and place them at the bottom of the pile, bringing their card to the top. Proper execution of this step is extremely important. If you do not place the cards above the spectator's chosen card at the bottom of the packet, the trick fails.

3 Now place the spectator's card on the table by itself and hold the rest of the cards in your left hand. Use your thumb to slide across the first card into your right hand. In this example, it's the Nine of Diamonds.

4 Then turn over the card in your right hand and the entire deck as shown. This creates the illusion that both cards in your hand are the same color when in reality they are both different.

5 After apparently showing the backs of the cards, turn both piles face up again. Then place the card in your right hand and the top card in the deck on the table face up. Please note: it is important that you do not show the bottom of the top card, as it will be the opposite color. Then repeat this process. Push the top card into your right hand and turn it over with the deck, again creating the impression that all the cards in your hand are the same color.

6 Repeat Step 5 until you have no more cards left. Then tell the spectator to turn over their card and reveal that it has a different color back to all the other cards!

A BET THAT NO ONE WILL REFUSE

EFFECT:

The magician explains that he knows a secret technique used by gamblers to win millions of dollars in casinos. This technique allows him to locate any card he likes just by feeling the deck. The spectator chooses a card and the magician bets the spectator he can find it. The trick seems to go wrong, and just when the spectator thinks he has won the bet, the magician locates the spectator's card!

PREPARATION:

You need a deck of cards.

PERFORMANCE:

Watch Video

1 Allow the spectator to shuffle the cards up as much as they like. Then instruct them to take around one-third of the deck and give the other two-thirds of the cards to you.

2 Now tell your spectator to shuffle the packet in their hand even more and then to remember the top card in that pile. There could not be a fairer way to select a card. In this example, the spectator is remembering the King of Hearts.

3 As they do this, remember the bottom card in your pile. This will be your Key Card. In this case, it is the Nine of Spades.

4   Have your spectator return their selection to the top of their pile. Then instruct them to place their packet on top of your packet.

5   Then to make things fair, tell your spectator to cut the cards in half and complete the cut. Of course, this means that their selection is now under your Key Card! Let the spectator cut the cards three more times to properly lose it in the deck. Remember, as explained earlier in the "Keep A Poker Face or I'll Guess Your Card" effect, cutting the cards does not change the order of the deck. It just changes what cards are on the top and bottom of the pile.

6, 7, 8 Mention that you are going to find their card using a rare technique that only the most elite gamblers are aware of. Take the deck back and deal cards one by one face-up onto the table. Keep talking about how this technique cannot fail, and soon you will find their card.

Here is where the magic begins. When you come across your Key Card, you know that the one after it is their selection. In this example, our Key Card is the Nine of Spades, meaning the card after it, the King of Hearts, is their selection. However, deal three more cards *past* their selection and then say, "I'm so certain this has worked, I bet you that the next card that I turn over will be yours." Of course, your spectator thinks that you've got the trick wrong since you've already dealt their card out onto the table.

9, 10 Once they take you up on the bet, move your hand to the top of the deck as if you are going to turn the next card over. Then hesitate and move your hand back to the table and turn over their card! Finish by saying "I told you, this technique always works!"

PRO TIP:

You can perform this trick alongside effects taught earlier such as "The Lazy Man's Card Trick" (page 18) and "Become a Master Pickpocket!" (page 32). All three tricks complement each other since they demonstrate an apparent high level of skill and mastery over playing cards.

The More You Look, the Less You See.

COIN TRICKS

As the name suggests, coin magic is the art of manipulating coins to entertain and bewilder your audience. It happens in a close-up setting and usually involves the performer vanishing, producing, and teleporting coins between their hands. I've selected seven coin tricks that are easy to do and look really impressive. You can perform them in practically any situation to break the ice, showcase your skill, and amaze your friends.

THE FRENCH DROP VANISH

EFFECT:

The magician makes a coin vanish while transferring it between his hands. The coin then appears behind the spectator's ear. This effect is a classic in coin magic and is certainly one of "the oldest tricks in the book." As you're about to find out, French Drop vanish is a dynamic sleight that can be utilized to vanish pretty much any small object. However, I'd recommend that you start off learning it with coins as they tend to be the easiest prop to vanish. Nevertheless, once you have mastered the technique you'll be able to make sweets, pen lids, dice and most other tiny objects disappear!

PREPARATION:

All you need is one large coin. Sitting in front of a mirror will also be useful so that you can see what the vanish looks like from the spectator's point of view.

PERFORMANCE:

1 Hold the coin in your non-dominant hand between the tip of your middle finger and thumb. Make sure your hand is palm up.

2 With your dominant hand, come in as if you are taking the coin. Your thumb should pass under the coin while your other fingers pass over it.

Once your hand completely covers the coin, use your dominant thumb to jog your other thumb (that is supporting the coin) to the side. This will cause the coin to fall into your non-dominant hand.

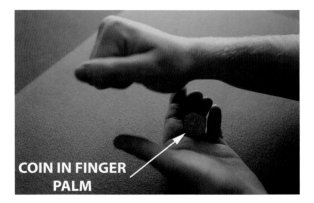

COIN IN FINGER PALM

Continue to close your dominant hand into a complete fist. This will create the illusion that it contains the coin.

6 At the same time, curl your fingers in your non-dominant hand around the coin. This is called a "finger palm." This will allow you to rotate your wrist so that the palm of your hand faces the table; adding to the illusion that the coin is in your other hand.

7 Pull your non-dominant hand holding the coin away while keeping your eyes focused on your empty hand. Suddenly, blow on your closed fist and then open it up to reveal that the coin has gone. Then look at your spectator inquisitively. Move the hand holding the coin behind their ear and produce it.

PRO TIP:

To make the French Drop vanish as natural as possible, practice actually taking the coin a few times with your dominant hand. Then try and mimic this action when you perform the vanish.

THE INSTANT COIN VANISH

EFFECT:

The magician displays a coin on his open palm. He taps the coin three times with a pen and on the third tap the coin instantly vanishes.

PREPARATION:

You will need a coin and a pen.

PRO TIP:

If you are looking to get into close up magic, then this effect is a "must learn" since it can be performed even while surrounded by spectators and looks like a camera trick in real life!

PERFORMANCE:

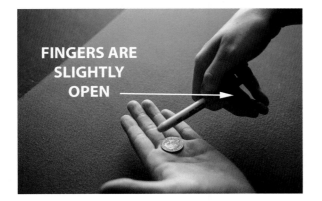

1 Place the coin in your left hand so that it is positioned near the base of your middle finger and ring finger. Then take the pen and hold it in your right hand. One end of the pen should be touching the coin and the other end should be held between your thumb and index finger.

2 Importantly, you want your middle, ring, and pinkie fingers to all be slightly open. Take a look at the picture above for a visual reference.

3 Tap the face of the coin twice with the pen. As the pen moves downwards for the third tap, move your left hand (that is holding the coin) upwards fast enough so that the coin is tossed in the air.

4 Catch the coin in your right hand with your middle, ring, and pinkie fingers. It will look as if the coin has magically disappeared.

PRO TIP:

Here is some advice to help you learn this move faster. When tossing the coin, try and aim for your right-hand fingers that are going to catch it. This means you should avoid throwing the coin directly upwards and instead angle the toss slightly to the right. I recommend that you isolate this move and practice it over and over again by itself. It is surprisingly simple once you get the hang of it! You can also do this vanish with any other small object such as a ring, sweet, or pen lid.

TABLE RUB

EFFECT:

The magician rubs a coin through a solid table. This is a fantastic impromptu trick that you can do anytime you have a table and a coin!

PREPARATION:

You need a coin. Any size will do, but bigger coins tend to be easier to use. You'll also need a table surface to perform on.

PERFORMANCE:

1 Place the coin onto the table. You want it to be around 5 inches from its edge.

2 Cover the coin with your right hand so that the middle of your fingers are on top of it.

3, 4 From here, you are going to make small circular rubbing motions with your hand. The first half of the circular rub will involve moving your hand towards your chest. As you do this, press down on the coin, and it will move backwards from your fingers to your palm. The second half of the circular motion involves moving your hand away from you. Of course, don't touch the coin when moving your hand away.

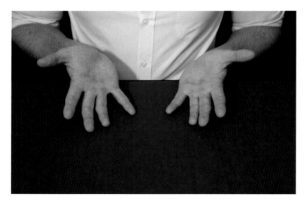

PRO TIP:

Once you understand the technique behind this effect, you'll realize just how easy it is to do. However, you need to make sure that the surface you are using is soft or your spectators will hear the coin being dragged backwards.

5 As you will see, this allows you to drag the coin backwards under the guise of rubbing it into the table. Keep doing this until the coin falls off the table onto your lap!

COIN THROUGH HAND

EFFECT:

The magician passes a coin straight through his hand. While this seems impossible, with a little bit of showmanship and misdirection, I'll teach you exactly how to pull off this mesmerizing trick.

PREPARATION:

A You will need two identical coins; the bigger, the better. This trick works especially well at the table with your spectators sitting directly opposite you.

PRO TIP:

If you don't have a table to perform this on, then ask the spectator to hold out their hand as a makeshift table. The coin will go through your hand and land on theirs!

B Hide one coin between the fleshy part of your thumb and index finger of your right hand. This is known as a "thumb clip." The lovely thing about the thumb clip is you can wiggle all your fingers openly and display the back of your hand naturally, creating the illusion that you are not hiding anything.

C Flip over this hand, so that your palm is facing down. Your spectators will have no idea that the coin is there. You are now ready to perform.

PERFORMANCE:

1 Sit down at the table and showcase the second coin to your spectators. Make sure that your hand hiding the first coin is relaxed and in a natural position. From here, you are going to pretend to push the other coin through your hand. Hold the second coin in your left hand between your thumb and first three fingers. Rotate the coin to a vertical position and place it onto the back of your right hand.

2 Tap the coin onto your skin a couple of times as if you are trying to push it through. On the third tap, slide your first three fingers down over the coin so that it is completely covered.

3 As soon as the coin is entirely hidden from view, release the other coin from the thumb clip. It will fall down onto the table and create the impossible illusion that the coin has passed straight through your hand.

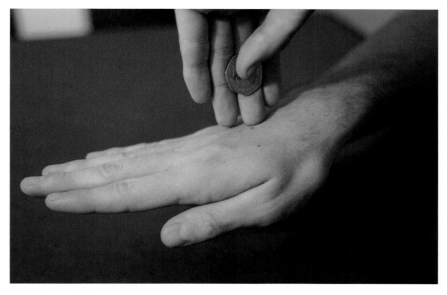

4 At this point, there will be one coin on the table and one coin hidden behind your fingers. Use your thumb to slide the coin behind your fingers upwards by around an inch. From here, you can close your bottom three fingers around the coin (this is known as a "finger palm").

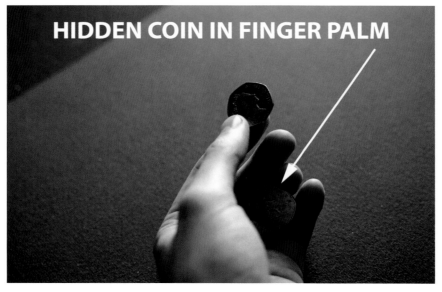

HIDDEN COIN IN FINGER PALM

5 Use the same hand to pick up the coin from the table, which will distract spectators from the other coin that you are cupping behind your bottom three fingers. Simply ditch the hidden coin in your pocket or on your lap, and you'll be completely clean.

JUMPING HANDS

EFFECT:

The magician places a coin in his hand. He tells the spectator not to blink or they will miss the magic! He turns his hands over quickly, and when he opens them again, the coin has teleported to his other hand.

PREPARATION:

You're going to need one coin and a flat surface to perform on. When learning this move, begin by using a large coin. However, once you have mastered the technique, you'll be able to use a coin of any size.

PERFORMANCE:

1 Begin by placing the coin on the edge of your left hand as shown. Both hands need to be palm up.

2 Next, turn both of your hands over as fast as possible so that they are palm down on the table. Due to the positioning of the coin in your left hand, when you flip your hands over, the coin will fly across and land under your right hand. This happens so quickly that the spectator will not be able to see the coin move.

PRO TIP:

This trick fully embodies the old adage "the hand is quicker than the eye." To practice, just sit down at a table and repeat the steps outlined above over and over again. You'll be able to get the hang of this pretty quickly. I prefer to do this on soft surfaces like a card mat or tablecloth as they reduce the sound of the coins hitting the table.

3 From here, you can slowly raise both hands and reveal that the coin has teleported into your other hand.

COIN MATRIX

PREPARATION:

A This trick requires five coins and a table. Place four of the coins in a square shape about six inches away from each other.

B The final coin should be on the side of the table and will be covered with the base of your right palm. Your spectator will have no idea that the coin is there.

PERFORMANCE:

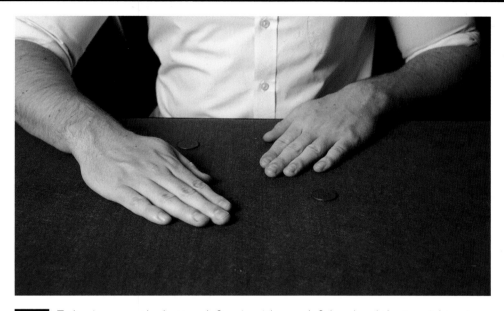

1 To begin, cover the bottom left coin with your left hand and the top right coin with your right hand. However, as you move your right hand up to cover the coin, drag the extra coin along the table with your hand.

2 Now move your right hand sideways revealing both coins. At the same time, move your left hand sideways but drag the coin that is underneath it along, too. If both moves are done simultaneously, it will look as if the bottom left-hand coin has jumped to the top right-hand corner.

3 We are going to repeat this process two more times, just with different coins. Drag your left hand (which has a hidden coin under it) to the top right-hand pile of coins. Simultaneously, move your right hand to the bottom right-hand corner and cover the single coin that is resting there.

4 Similar to previous steps, move your left hand away, revealing three coins while your right-hand drags the bottom right coin to the side.

5 Finally, cover up the top left coin with your left hand and the top right pile with your right hand (of course dragging the hidden coin along with it).

6 Move both hands to the side, revealing that all four coins have teleported to the top right corner. You should have a hidden coin under your left hand. Just drag this backwards until it falls off the edge of the table onto your lap.

COIN FROM NOWHERE

EFFECT:

The magician shows both hands empty. He then produces a coin from nowhere.
Everything can be examined—you have nothing to hide!

PREPARATION:

All you need is a coin.

PERFORMANCE:

1 Take a coin and clip it in between the thumb and index finger of your right hand. This is known as a "thumb clip."

2 Rotate your hand so that it is palm down and at a slight angle where your pinkie finger is closer to the ground than your thumb. This will hide the coin from your spectators.

PRO TIP:

This is a really good opener that can be used to begin your coin tricks. Once you have produced the coin, you can then go on to do anything you like (such as vanishing it, pushing it through your hands, or even making it teleport!)

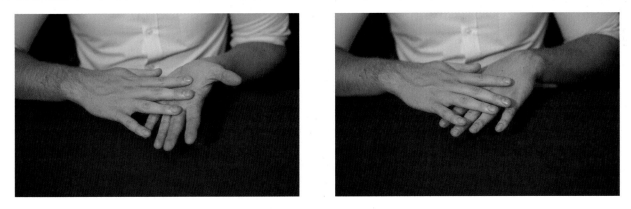

3, 4 Now use your right hand and brush the front and back of your left hand cleanly. This creates the deceptive illusion that you have nothing to hide.

5 Next, angle your hand downward, so your fingertips are pointing towards the ground. Then curl your fingers in. This will allow the coin to fall from its clipped position onto your fingertips as shown.

6 From here, just use your thumb to push the coin outwards to produce it.

JW GRIP PRODUCTION

EFFECT:

Everyone dreams of being able to reach into thin air and pluck out money. Well the JW Grip Production will enable you to do just that. The magician shows his hand clean and empty. He then suddenly produces a coin from nowhere. This is a fun trick that you can learn in a matter of seconds, yet it fools people every time.

PRO TIP:

Practice this in front of the mirror, and you'll be able to see it from the spectator's point of view. You can also combine this move with the French Drop vanish to create a two-phased trick! You can also use this trick to produce a ring. In the performance video I produced a ring and placed it onto my finger at the same time—definitely give this cool effect a go, too!

PREPARATION:

A To begin, you need to get the coin into what is known as "JW Grip." Place the coin horizontally in the middle of your index finger on your right hand as shown. You want to curl your finger around the coin so that it doesn't fall down onto the floor.

B You now need to move your other fingers so that the spectators standing in front of you cannot see the coin. Place your middle finger directly against the edge of the coin, while your ring and pinkie fingers are pulled back, opening up your hand. From a frontal view, it will look as if there is nothing in your hand.

PERFORMANCE:

1 With the coin in JW grip, show your spectators that your hand is empty. Then take your thumb and contact the edge of the coin that is closest to yourself.

2, 3, 4 Pull the coin down and out, moving it into view so that it rests between your thumb and index finger. This is one of the best ways to show your hand empty, and then moments later produce a coin.

MENTALISM

This next section is going to give you the ability to divine what a spectator is thinking about just by looking at them. If you've ever wanted to read someone's mind or plant a thought in your friend's head, then study these pages very carefully. You'll learn to predict the future, control someone's decisions, do complex mathematical calculations faster than a calculator, and so much more! I've also made sure that all of these tricks are easy to learn; so, combine them with a touch of showmanship and you'll be blowing people's minds in no time at all.

Are you excited?
Yes?
How did I know that?

KNOW WHAT CARD YOUR SPECTATOR IS THINKING OF

EFFECT:

The spectator shuffles the cards, chooses one, and returns it into the deck. Then, reading the spectator's body language, the magician can tell exactly what card they picked.

PREPARATION:

This trick can be done with a borrowed, shuffled deck of cards. The secret is diabolically simple—you're going to peek at the spectator's card in the most ingenious way and then pretend to "read their body language" to work out what their card is. Let me show you how.

2 Now turn the deck back over and ask your spectator to pick a card.

PERFORMANCE:

Watch Video

1 Let the spectator mix up the cards as much as possible. Once they are satisfied, take the deck back. You now need to peak at the bottom card. There are two ways to do this—in the performance video I rotated the cards 180 degrees and tilted them up just enough to see what the bottom card was. However, another way to do it is to casually turn over the deck to show that it is actually mixed. As you do this, glance at the bottom card, and remember it. This will be your Key Card. In this case, it is the Two of Diamonds.

PRO TIP:

If you are looking for a trick that will impress your friends and make you the life of the party, then look no further. This magic trick is perfect to do at social gatherings, networking events, or any situation where you have a large group of people that you want to impress. It hits hard, yet cannot go wrong, making it my go-to mentalism effect.

SPECTATOR'S SELECTION

DEALING CARDS DOWN

3 Once they have done this, begin to deal small piles of cards from the top of the deck onto the table.

4 Tell your spectator to say stop whenever they like. Once they say stop, let them place their selection on top of the cards that are on the table.

5 Finally, put the rest of the cards in your hand on top of the deck. Now instruct your spectator to cut the cards as many times as they please. Remember—cutting the cards does not change the order of the deck, it only changes the position of the top and bottom card.

Once they have cut the cards three or four times, dramatically pause for a few seconds and confirm with the spectator that you do not know *what* their card is, nor do you know *where* it is in the deck. They shuffled the cards, returned it into the pack wherever they liked and then cut it multiple times! This couldn't be any fairer.

6   Now pick up the deck and run through it. Find the Key Card (in this case it's the Two of Diamonds) and the card above it will be their selection. Remember what their card is.

As you do this, say, "Look I could go through the deck like this and try to find your card. However, I want to take this one step further and read your mind." Put the cards down, pause, and look at them. You want to build this moment up as much as possible. Now, you need a touch of showmanship to really sell the illusion that you are reading their mind. Here is how I present it. Let's say they were thinking of the Five of Spades, I would say something like this:

"Okay, I want you to keep an absolute poker face and give nothing away. Relax your shoulders and look at me directly in the eyes. Now slowly count from 1 to 10 for me. Ah, you paused on the four and five. Look at me . . . Yes, it's definitely a five. Now think of the suit. Really picture it in front of you. Yes, that's good. Try and send it to me in your mind. Okay, it's definitely black. . . . it is the Five of Spades!"

PRO TIP:

This effect relies on a very simple premise—you peek at their card and then reveal what it is. Therefore, when practicing, make sure you rehearse what you are going to say when "reading their mind." Use my example above as a template and then add in extra lines that suit your performance style.

If the spectator happens to cut directly between your Key Card and their selection, then fear not! This trick will still work perfectly. This scenario would result in the Key Card being on the bottom of the deck and their card being placed on the top. This means, when you turn the deck over, you will see your Key Card and instantly know that the card at the other end of the deck will be their selection.

THE MIND READING TEST: CONTROL YOUR SPECTATOR'S DECISIONS

EFFECT:

The magician tells the spectator that he is going to subconsciously influence their decision. He lays out three cards on the table. One card is red, one card is blue, and the other is yellow. He tells the spectator to choose any card they like—this seems like a free choice. The spectator chooses the yellow card. The magician turns over all three cards and the yellow card is the only one that says, "You will choose this card."

PREPARATION:

A This is a beautiful effect that creates the illusion that you are controlling your spectator's decisions. It utilizes an old principle in magic known as having "multiple outs." In the context of this trick, you have three different predictions, each one corresponding to the different cards on the table. This means regardless of what card the spectator selects, you will always have a prediction that claims you knew what they were going to do!

B Take three cards (these can be bits of paper if you like) and color one in red, one in yellow and one in blue.

C On the back of the yellow card write "You will choose this card."

D Now take a pencil and write "You will choose the blue card" on the side.

E Finally, take an envelope and on the back of it write "You will choose red." Then place all three cards into the envelope and leave it face-up on the table. You are ready to begin.

PRO TIP:

This trick is a good opener because it cannot go wrong, is easy to do, and looks very impressive. As such, consider opening your performance with this effect.

PERFORMANCE:

Explain to your spectator that you have the ability to influence their decisions. Open up the envelope making sure that you don't flash the prediction written on its underside. Place all three cards onto the table.

2 Give the pencil to your spectator and tell them to point to any card that they like.

If they point to the yellow card, turn over all three cards and reveal that the yellow card was the only one that says, "You will choose this card."

4 If they select the blue card, snap your fingers and tell them to look at what is written on the side of the pencil that they are holding. Of course, it will read "You will choose the blue card."

5 If they decide to go with the red card, then put all three cards back into the envelope. Then turn the envelope over and reveal that you predicted that they will choose the red card. As you can see, this is a powerful quick trick that cannot go wrong. Enjoy using it to blow people's minds!

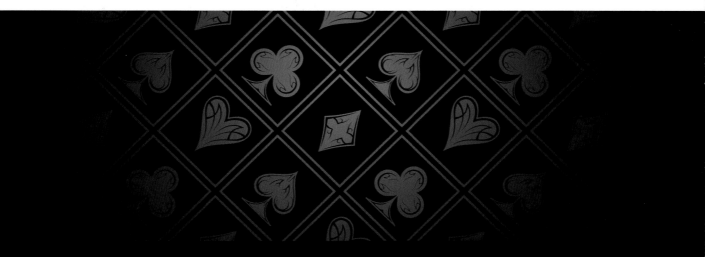

BECOME A MATHEMATICAL GENIUS

This trick is so powerful that magicians often close their stage shows (in front of thousands of people) with it. Yes . . . it is that good! The spectator can name any number between twenty and ninety-nine. In this case, the spectator chooses forty-five. In a matter of seconds, the magician writes down sixteen numbers in a grid.

All the numbers in each row, column, and diagonal add up to forty-five. So do the outer four numbers and the middle four numbers. Your spectators will think you are a mathematical genius. If only they knew how simple this trick actually is.

PREPARATION:

All you need is a number selected between twenty-two and ninety-nine and then a piece of paper to draw the magic square on.

PERFORMANCE:

	1	12	7
11	8		2
5	10	3	
4		6	9

1 Draw out a 4 × 4 grid onto your paper and then ask the spectator to pick a number between twenty-two and ninety-nine. Next, write down the numbers above into the grid. These numbers never change.

A	1	12	7
11	8	D	2
5	10	3	C
4	B	6	9

42	1	12	7
11	8	41	2
5	10	3	44
4	43	6	9

2 You will notice that there are four blank spots on the grid. We will label them A, B, C, and D. These blank spots change depending on what number the spectator chooses.

3 For spot A, subtract 20 from the spectator's number. For spot B, add one to the number in A. For spot C, add one to the number in B. For spot D, subtract 1 from the number in A. And that's it! Add up the rows, columns, diagonals, corners and they will all make your spectators chosen number.

For example, if the spectator picks the number sixty-two, begin by writing out all of the numbers that will never change first, then do the following equations.

Spot A: 62—20 = 42
Spot B: 42 + 1 = 43
Spot C: 43 + 1 = 44
Spot D: 42—1 = 41

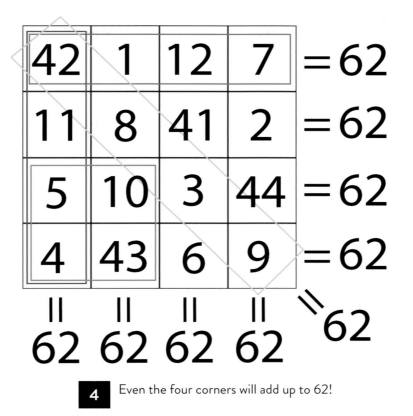

4 Even the four corners will add up to 62!

PRO TIP:

Once you have memorized the method behind this trick, really focus on *how* you present it. You could create a backstory about how you once hit your head and fell into a deep sleep. When you woke up, your brain allowed you to do complex calculations much faster than a calculator. Then demonstrate your strange ability by doing this trick.

If you want to take this magic trick to the next level, then combine it with the center tear (taught on page 84). This will allow you to ask the spectator to think of a number, then secretly find out what that number is after they write it down. Next, create the magic square based on their number. Finally, point to your magic square and say, "If I have done this correctly, one of these numbers corresponds to the one you are thinking of!" Of course, none of the numbers in the magic square match their one, and the spectator will assume you have got the trick wrong. Then ask them what their number is, and reveal that all the rows, columns, and diagonals add up to it!

PUT A THOUGHT IN A SPECTATOR'S MIND

EFFECT:

The magician tries to put a thought in the spectator's mind. He asks the spectator to think of a country and animal, and correctly guesses what the spectator is thinking of.

PREPARATION:

Just learn the script below. The trick is pretty much self-working!

PRO TIP:

This trick works around 90 percent of the time. The mathematical section of the trick always forces the spectator to pick the number 4. This means they will choose the letter D and subsequently pick Denmark (as it is the only European country that begins with D). When asking them to think of an animal that begins with E, tell them to do it quickly and mention that the animal can be "big or small." This will influence them to select an Elephant almost every time.

PERFORMANCE:

Say the following to your spectator:

1. *Think of any number from 1 to 10.*
2. *Now multiply this number by 9 [give them time to do this].*
3. *If the number you are thinking of has two-digits, then add both digits together. For example, if you were thinking of 24, you will a 2 + 4 giving you the number 6.*
4. *Subtract 5 from this new number.*
5. *Now match that number to its corresponding letter in the alphabet. For example, "1" matches with "A", "2" matches with "B", "3" matches with "C," etc.*
6. *Do you have a letter? Brilliant, let's continue!*
7. *Now think of a European country that starts with that letter [pause while they think of it].*
8. *Now go to the second letter in that country's name and think of an animal (big or small) whose name begins with that letter.*
9. *Now think of the color of that animal.*
10. *[Look at your spectator inquisitively].*
11. *Say "No, no, no . . . you've got this all wrong. There are NO GRAY ELEPHANTS IN DENMARK!"*

THE CIRCLE ROUTINE

EFFECT:

The magician's prediction perfectly matches a shape that was fairly chosen by the spectator. This trick is a true reputation maker that your spectators are going to remember for years to come.

PRO TIP:

If your spectator happens to not have any change, or only has a couple of coins, then just add your own money. Casually reach into your pocket and grab some of your own coinage and continue with the trick as normal.

PREPARATION:

A On a piece of paper, write down "You will pick the circle." This is your prediction; fold it up and place it on the table.

B Next, take a coin (any type of coin will work) and draw a circle on one side of it using a permanent marker.

C Finger palm this coin by curling the middle and ring finger of your right hand around it. Make sure the side of the coin that has no circle drawn on it is facing your fingers. You are now ready to begin.

PERFORMANCE:

1 Place the prediction face down on the table. Then ask your spectator if you can borrow a few coins. Let them reach into their pocket and pull out some change.

2 Let them dump the money out on the table. Then reach over to take it with your right hand. As you do so, secretly drop the palmed coin onto their change. If you drag all of the change towards you as you deposit the coin, then the spectator will not hear it clink onto the pile. This is because the big action of moving the coins causes them to tap together, hiding the little sound of you covertly dropping your extra coin.

3 Place all the money on the table, making sure the circle on your coin remains face down so the spectator cannot see it. Drag five coins to the side, including your gimmicked one. Now ask the spectator to name five shapes. Draw one shape on each coin. They will inevitably say "Circle." Make sure you draw the circle on your gimmicked coin. This will mean that all the coins have random shapes on them, but your coin, unbeknownst to the spectator, will have two circles on it.

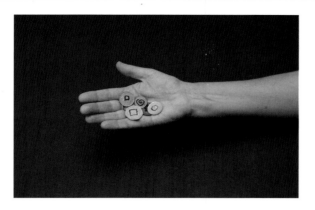

4 Place the coins in the spectator's hand and tell them to shake them up.

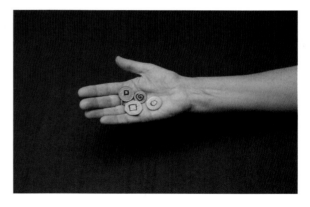

5 When the spectator opens their hands, some coins will have shapes on them and other coins will not since they have flipped over.

6 Eliminate any coins that do not have any shapes on them.

7 Keep doing this until you have just one coin left. The final coin will always be your gimmicked coin because it has a circle on both sides meaning it can *never* be eliminated.

8 Take the final coin out of your spectator's hand and place it on the table. Then open your prediction and reveal that you knew they would choose the coin with a circle on it all along.

PRO TIP:

One of the reasons this mentalism effect is so powerful is because it happens in the spectator's hands. They decide what shapes to use, they shake the coins up themselves, and they eliminate the coins. Yet you can correctly guess the outcome 100 percent of the time! I like to begin this effect by saying, "Last night I had a strange dream that you were going to choose a particular shape. So, I got up and wrote down what shape I dreamt you would pick [point to your prediction]. Let's see if my dream was correct."

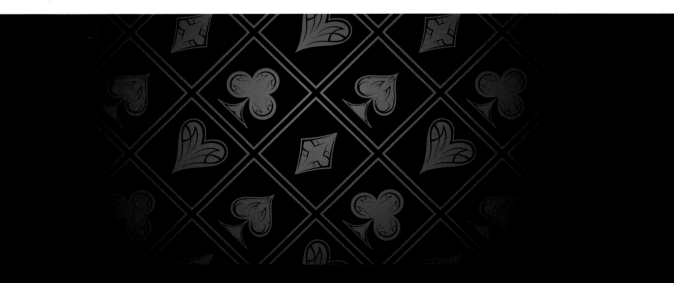

PREDICT THE FUTURE

EFFECT:

The magician places a prediction into an envelope and then places the envelope on the table. The spectator deals cards onto the table and randomly stops at the Ace of Spades. The magician then opens his prediction and pulls out the Six of Clubs—the wrong card! He then turns the Six of Clubs over and on the back it says, "Check My Phone." The magician unlocks their phone and the last picture on their photos app is a picture of the Ace of Spades!

PREPARATION:

A Before the trick begins, take a photograph of the Ace of Spades on your phone.

B Now place the Ace of Spades ninth from the top of the deck. Then take another playing card (it doesn't matter what value) and write "Check My Phone" on its back. To make this easier to read, I've written this message on a tiny piece of paper and then stuck it onto the card directly. This is going to be your fake prediction.

C Place the card into an envelope and you are ready to begin.

PERFORMANCE:

1 Place the envelope onto the table, explaining that inside you have a prediction. Give the spectator the deck and then tell them to think of a number between ten and twenty. Let's just say they think of the number twelve. Tell them to deal down twelve cards.

2 There should now be a pile of cards that they have just dealt onto the table. Tell them to pick up this pile and then to make things even more random, take the two digits of the number they thought of and add them together. They thought of twelve, so tell them to deal down three cards from the pile. The next card will be their "randomly selected chosen card."

3 When they turn it over, it will be the Ace of Spades. Now point to your prediction. Everyone will be expecting you to pull out a matching card but instead you will remove the Six of Clubs. This is a powerful moment—act as if the trick has gone wrong and look confused.

4 Then turn over the card and reveal that it says, "Check My Phone."

5 Slowly open up your phone and reveal that you knew all along that they would select the Ace of Spades.

PRO TIP:

There are so many other possible ways to reveal the spectator's chosen card—it doesn't just have to be a prediction that you made on your phone earlier. For example, you could have a matching card in your top pocket, or in your wallet have a note that says, "You will choose the Ace of Spades." You could even write "Ace of Spades" on your arm and then roll up your sleeve when it's time to reveal it. Get creative—your imagination is the only limitation!

KNOW WHAT WORD YOUR SPECTATOR IS THINKING OF

EFFECT:

The spectator thinks of any word they like. The magician then uses a combination of throat reading and body language analysis to correctly guess what that word is. This effect is often referred to as the "holy grail" of mentalism since it epitomizes mind reading in its most direct and straightforward form. This effect uses a technique that magicians call the "center tear."

PREPARATION:

All you need is a piece of paper no bigger than four inches by four inches (sticky notes work really well).

2 The spectator now has a word that you couldn't possibly know. Tell them that to make things fair, you want someone else in the room to know what that word is. This way, your spectator cannot suddenly change their mind and cheat! Take out your paper and tell them to write down their word in the circle and show it to their friend.

PERFORMANCE:

1 Draw a circle in the middle of the paper big enough for the spectator to write a word in as shown. Begin by asking the spectator to think of a memory that is important to them. Then ask them to think of any word that is related to that memory. For example, the spectator might think of a time they went swimming and so the word they think of is "Water."

3 Turn around as they do this. Once they are done, tell them to fold the paper in half and then in half again, so that there is no way you can see it. Once this is completed, turn back around.

4 Take the folded paper and explain that you are going to tear it up to get rid of any evidence of the word. Hold the paper in your right hand. You will be able to see that two edges are open and two edges have folds in them. Rotate the paper so that the folded edges are positioned along the top and right-hand side as shown.

5 Tear the paper down the middle so that you have two pieces.

6 Put the piece in your right hand on top of the piece in your left hand (so that the right-hand strip is closer to you).

Rotate both pieces 90 degrees clockwise and then make another tear down the middle.

7 Again, place the pieces in your right hand on top of the pieces in your left hand. Now, here is the magic part! Despite it looking like you've torn up all the paper, your spectator's word is actually unharmed. It is inside the strip of paper closest to you on top of the pile. Therefore, use your right thumb to pull this piece of paper into the palm of your hand and then dump the rest of the pieces on the table.

8 All you need to do is secretly open this paper and glimpse at what their word is. You can do this under the table, or by distracting your spectators by telling them to burn the other bits of paper. You can even just open it up in your hand, quickly glance down and read it, and then look back up and continue with the trick!

From here on, the rest of the trick is just showmanship. Pretend to read their mind by looking at their body language and guess what word they are thinking of!

PRO TIP:

Once you know what their word is, you can utilize something that magicians call "cold reading." This is where you make a series of high-probability guesses based on their word. For example, if their word was "school" you could say the following.

"Okay, really think of your memory. Yes, that's good. Picture it in front of you. Now I'm sensing that this happened quite a long time ago. Yes, and you are surrounded by quite a lot of other people who were all your age. Hmm, this memory that you are thinking of is slightly embarrassing, but you look back at it now and laugh! Think of the first letter in your word. It begins with S, doesn't it? Now picture the entire word in front of you. Is your word 'school'?"

As you can see from the passage above, I've just made some generic assumptions about schools which are almost always going to be correct. However, this intensifies the illusion that I am reading their mind. To practice this technique, jot down a few words onto some paper and then try and come up with some cold reading patter similar to that shown above.

WALLET PREDICTION

EFFECT:

The spectator chooses any card they like. The magician then opens up his wallet, and inside is a prediction that correctly names the spectator's card.

PRO TIP:

You can pair this trick with the "Become A Master Pickpocket!" effect taught on page 32. Begin with this illusion by bringing out your wallet and correctly predicting your spectators card. Then transition into the pickpocket routine by pointing to your wallet and saying something like, "Now, this reminds me of a little known pickpocketing technique that I spent several years trying to master. Would you like to see it?" This will make your routine flow naturally, complementing the structure of your overall performance.

B   Then remove the Seven of Hearts from the deck and place it facedown near the edge of the table. Put your wallet on top of the seven and you're ready to begin.

PREPARATION:

A   Before you begin, take a piece of paper and write down "You will choose the Seven of Hearts." Place this inside your wallet as your prediction.

PERFORMANCE:

1   Give the cards to the spectator so that they can shuffle them up. Once they are happy, tell them to deal the cards face down onto the table one by one. Wherever they stop dealing will be their card.

**THE TOP CARD UNDER THE WALLET
IS NOW THE 7 OF HEARTS**

Once the spectator has stopped, you are going to say, "To make things even more fair, we are going to mark your card with my wallet so that no one can change it." Pick up your wallet by sliding it off the table with the Seven of Hearts hidden beneath it. Then place both the wallet and the Seven onto the pile of cards that the spectator has just dealt. This automatically changes the top card to the Seven of Hearts.

Now distract your spectator for a few moments. Confirm that they could have chosen any card from the deck and that they were shuffled beforehand. Then point to your wallet, open it up and show that your prediction says, "You will choose the Seven of Hearts."

4 Then ask them to turn over the card they stopped at. Of course, it will perfectly match your prediction.

IMAGINATION DICE

EFFECT:

The spectator imagines rolling a pair of dice. The magician is then able to correctly guess what numbers the spectator imagined rolling to.

PREPARATION:

None.

PERFORMANCE:

Tell your spectator to roll two imaginary dice. Then have them:

1. Look at the first die and remember the (imaginary) number it rolled to.
2. Double this number.
3. Add 5 to it.
4. Multiply it by 5.
5. Add this number to the number they can see on the second die.
6. Say this final number out loud.

PRO TIP:

This is one of those effects that just works. When you eventually find out what their two numbers are, you want to upsell the effect by saying things like: "You never wrote anything down, so there is no possible way I could know what two numbers you are just THINKING of." Pause for a moment, and then reveal that they chose 6 and 4!

As the magician, all you need to do is subtract 25 from this final number and that will be the value of the two dies. For example, the spectator rolls the dice and imagines the numbers 6 and 4.

- 6 + 6 = 12
- 12 + 5 = 17
- 17 x 5 = 85
- 85 + 4 = 89
- 89 − 25 = 64.
- So, their numbers must be 6 and 4!

The More You Look, the Less You See.

MAGIC WITH EVERYDAY OBJECTS

Forks, rings, pens, rubber bands. These are all objects that we use or carry with us regularly, which is why it becomes particularly powerful when magicians can perform miracles with them. Being able to do magic with items that you can find lying around the house is very useful. It will move your skillset beyond just cards and coins, and enable you to amaze people with pretty much anything! The next few pages are packed with a diverse range of tricks, most of which you can learn in a matter of minutes. So, sit back and get ready because after reading this section, you're never going to look at a pen, a napkin, or a cell phone in the same way again!

LEVITATE A BANKNOTE

PREPARATION:

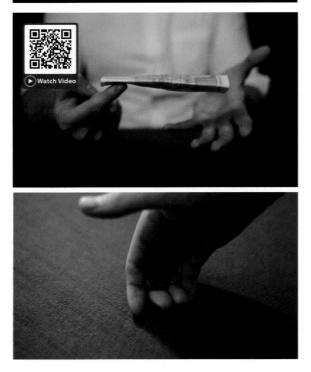

A   To do this trick you'll need a banknote and a coin. Before you begin, you want to finger palm the coin in your right hand. To do this, curl your middle finger around the coin and then let your hand rest naturally by your side.

PRO TIP:

When people see you balancing the note on your thumb, they usually suspect that there is a hidden wire keeping it suspended. To debunk this theory, take your free hand and wave it around the note showing that there are no hidden wires!

PERFORMANCE:

1   Tell your spectator that you are going to defy the laws of physics using their banknote. Take their note with your left hand and cleanly display it.

Now come in with your right hand and slip the coin behind the banknote in the action of grabbing it. This is very easy to do. Just place your thumb on the coin, straighten out your fingers, and slide the note behind the coin as shown.

2 Now fold the bottom third of the banknote upwards over the coin.

3 Next, fold the top third of the banknote downwards so that the coin is completely enveloped inside it.

4 From here, the trick just works. Place the heavier side of the note on your thumb and the added weight from the coin will mean that it will impossibly balance there when you remove all your fingers!

5 Once you have performed the levitation, rotate the note and secretly let the coin fall out into your hand. The note can now be handed out for inspection.

BEND A FORK WITH YOUR MIND

EFFECT:

The magician takes an ordinary fork and holds it at his fingertips. The fork slowly starts to bend. Suddenly, the fork breaks right before the spectator's eyes. Psychics have used this effect for years to showcase their supernatural gifts and ability to put "mind over matter." This effect also looks just as amazing when done with a spoon!

PREPARATION:

A Before you begin the trick, you need to pre-break the fork. Take the head of the fork in one hand and the handle of the fork in the other. Bend them up and down repeatedly until the fork breaks just below its head.

PRO TIP:

There are two questions that students usually ask when performing this trick. The first is "What is the best place to buy forks?" I recommend you go to a supermarket because forks tend to be cheaper there and break much more easily (making the pre-break easy to do.) Whatever you do, don't use an expensive silver fork that's worth a lot of money!

Secondly, students often ask how long they should make the "bending" phase of the trick last. I usually aim for around eight seconds since a slower bend is more visual and deceptive than a quick bend.

PERFORMANCE:

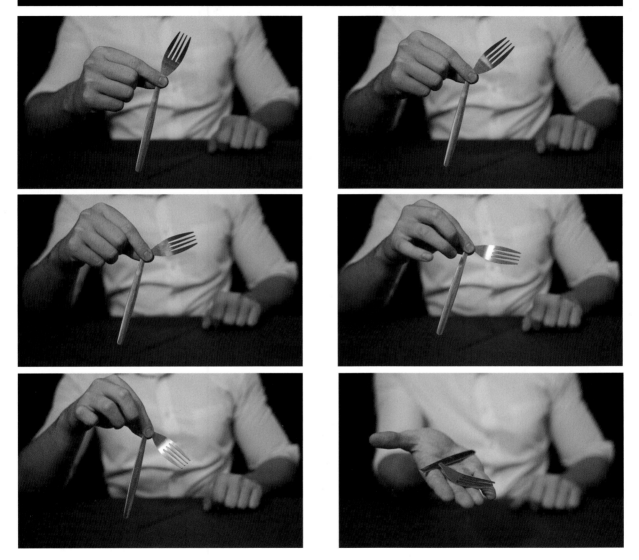

1, 2, 3, 4, 5, 6   Hold both pieces of the fork in between your thumb and index finger. This will make the fork look complete because your fingers are covering up the break.

Explain to your spectator that you are going to demonstrate your supernatural ability to bend metal with your mind. Focus on the fork and slowly loosen the grip with your fingers. Because the fork is pre-broken, both parts will begin to move separately; creating the illusion that it is bending. Then suddenly let the head of the fork fall onto the table. Now everything can be handed out for your spectators to inspect.

APPEARING TOOTHPICK

EFFECT:

The magician shows both of his hands completely empty and then plucks a toothpick out of thin air. Everything can be instantly examined.

PRO TIP:

You can also perform this trick as a vanish by reversing all the steps outlined above. So, begin by placing your hand in a fist to display the toothpick. Then suddenly open up your hand and the toothpick will vanish behind your thumb.

PERFORMANCE:

1 With the toothpick stuck to the back of your thumb display both hands to your spectator. Make sure that your fingers and thumbs are pointing upwards. This will create the deceptive illusion that your hands are completely empty.

PREPARATION:

A The secret to this effect is diabolically simple. Lick your right thumb in the space between the bottom of your nail and knuckle. Place the top of the toothpick onto this wetted area so that it runs down your thumb. The wetness will cause the toothpick to stick to your thumb.

2 In the action of moving your right hand towards the spectator, move your thumb down into the palm of your hand and then grab it with the rest of your fingers. This will instantly produce the toothpick from thin air.

3 The faster you perform this move, the more visual this trick will be. You can then instantly hand everything out to be inspected.

PRO TIP:

You can also perform this effect with a pencil. However, given that it weighs more than a toothpick, you will need to stick it to the back of your thumb with double-sided tape. Apart from that, the mechanics behind the trick are exactly the same as the toothpick version!

PHONE IN BOTTLE

EFFECT:

The magician takes his phone and pushes it straight inside a water bottle! He then cuts the phone out of the bottle and hands both items out to be inspected.

PREPARATION:

A You will need one large water bottle and a cell phone. Empty out the bottle, remove its label and then cut a large slit in the side of it that is longer than your phone. Please note that you should only do this trick if your mobile phone is waterproof.

PRO TIP:

I like to perform this effect with my phone screen on as it adds an extra layer of visual eye-candy to the trick and really helps the spectator "see" the phone penetrate straight through the bottle.

PERFORMANCE:

1 Hold the phone in your right hand and the water bottle in your left hand. You want the slit on the bottle to be facing your phone. This means from the front view, the slit is almost impossible to see since the curvature of the bottle hides it perfectly. Furthermore, because the bottle is transparent it looks as if you have nothing to hide, meaning your spectators will not suspect anything.

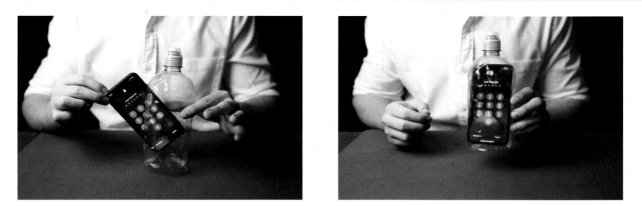

2, 3   Suddenly put the phone inside the bottle by pushing it through the slit in one quick motion.

4   Shake the bottle around to show that the phone is really inside. Then take a knife or some scissors and tell your spectator that you are going to cut it out of the bottle. Simply insert the knife into the existing slit and pretend to cut open the bottle. Then pull the phone out and hand everything out for inspection.

JUMPING RUBBER BAND

EFFECT:

A rubber band visually jumps between the magician's fingers. This is a quick, impressive, and hard hitting effect that looks like a camera trick! Watch the video performance to see just how visual it is.

PREPARATION:

You will need one small rubber band. However, you can use a larger rubber band and just wrap it around your fingers multiple times.

PRO TIP:

Try combining this effect with other rubber band tricks to create a routine. For example, you could begin with the "Linking Rubber Band" trick, then do the "Jumping Rubber Band" before finishing it off with the "Ring Up Rubber Band" illusion. Take a look at the "Presentation Tips" section on page 137 and the "Joke Bank" section to get a better idea on how to link particular tricks together naturally.

PERFORMANCE:

 Watch Video

1 Take the rubber band and place it around the index finger and middle finger on your right hand. Slide it down to the base of these fingers. You want this band to be relatively tight so keep looping it until it doesn't slack.

2 Using your left hand, pull back on the rubber band. This will create a large gap.

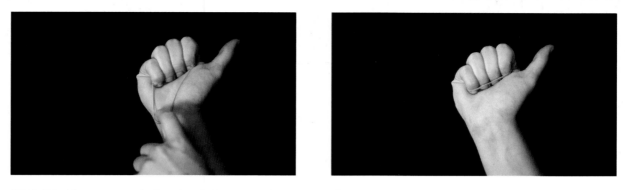

3, 4   Close your right hand and place your fingers into this gap. Then let go of the band with your left hand.

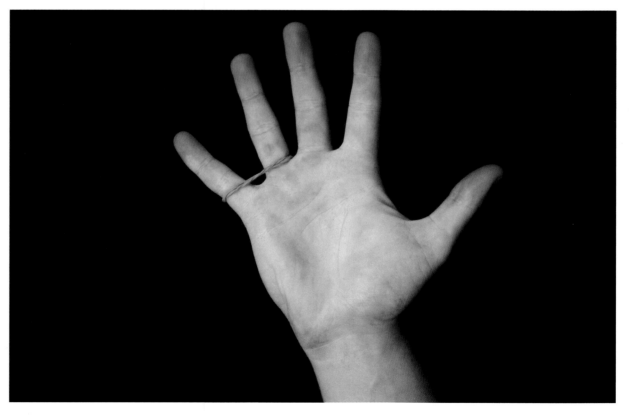

5   When you open up your hand, the rubber band will jump to your other two fingers. This is an incredibly visual magic trick.

DISAPPEARING PEN

EFFECT:

The magician picks up a pen and makes it disappear and then reappear moments later.

PREPARATION:

All you need is a pen.

PERFORMANCE:

1 Hold the pen horizontally in your right hand between your index finger, middle finger, and thumb. You need to make sure that your spectator is standing directly in front of you.

2 Move your left hand in front of the pen, keeping all of your fingers closed.

PRO TIP:

The key to this trick is becoming comfortable with The Flip Stick. Isolate that move and practice it by itself until you build up the muscle memory to perform it without thinking. Once you can execute The Flip Stick confidently, the rest of the trick becomes much easier.

From here, two things are going to happen at once. Extend the middle finger of your right hand slightly and pull back on the pen. This will cause it to fly into the palm of your right hand. This move is called "The Flip Stick."

At the same time, rotate your left hand around so that your palm is now facing away from you. From the spectator's point of view, the pen will have completely vanished.

6 To produce the pen, rotate your left hand back around so that its palm is facing you again.

7 Then use your thumb to push the pen back out into a horizontal position.

8 From here, you can move your left hand to the side and reveal the pen again.

CUP THROUGH TABLE

EFFECT:

The magician says he is going to push a coin through the table. He puts the coin under a cup, and accidentally pushes the cup through the table instead of the coin! This can be a devastatingly powerful effect that takes the spectator by surprise. If you are looking for a fun, easy trick to do at a restaurant or bar, then look no further!

PRO TIP:

The key to pulling off this effect is the misdirection segment. When "inspecting" the coin, you can say things like: "Ah yes, the coin needs to be heads up for this to work" or "Let me give the coin a magic blow so it can go through the table." Essentially, say anything that justifies the fact that you are inspecting the coin. As previously mentioned, this will take all the attention away from the cup and napkin, giving you plenty of misdirection for the ditch onto your lap.

PREPARATION:

A For this trick, you will need a cup, a coin, and a paper napkin. You also need to be sitting down at a table for this effect to work.

PERFORMANCE:

1 Show the coin, cup, and napkin to your spectators. Now take the cup and place its bottom edge onto the edge of the paper napkin. Roll the paper napkin around the cup, twisting it at the top.

2 Put the coin on the table. Then put the napkin (and cup) over the coin. Explain that when you lift up the cup, the coin will disappear!

3 Count to three and lift up the cup with your right hand. Of course, the coin will still be there.

4 Look confused and inspect the coin with your left hand, as if something is wrong with it. This will draw your spectator's attention to the coin and away from the cup.

5 As you look at the coin, move the cup and paper towards the edge of the table with your right hand. Once it is over the edge of the table, let the cup slide out onto your lap. You'll notice that the paper napkin will maintain the shape of the cup.

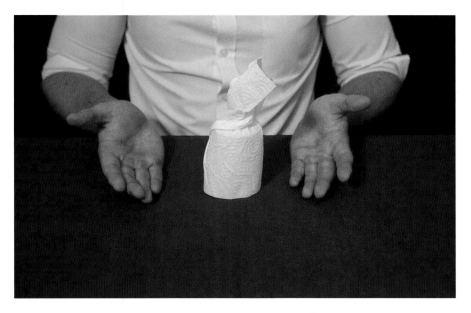

6 From here, tell your spectator that you are going to try again. Place the paper napkin over the coin. (Your spectators will assume the cup is still underneath it.)

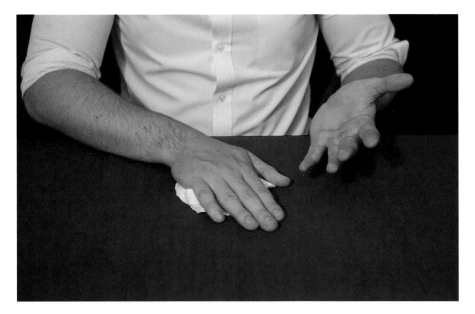

7 Then slam your hand down on the napkin and pretend to push the cup through the table.

ASHES ON ARM

PRO TIP:

This is a very powerful effect since it moves magic beyond just being a "card trick" and into the realm of physicality where the final effect becomes something material and tangible. You can have a lot of fun playing around with your presentation of this illusion. For example, you could showcase it as your supernatural ability to control the elements, or as a science experiment that always works but you don't know why.

PREPARATION:

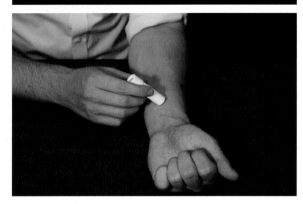

A This trick requires a deck of cards, an ashtray, some lip balm, matches, and some paper. Before you begin the trick, take the lip balm and draw a seven and diamond onto your wrist. Since the lip balm is transparent, the spectator will be unaware that you have the Seven of Diamonds etched into your arm.

B Now place the Seven of Diamonds on top of the deck.

PERFORMANCE:

1 Explain to your spectator that you are going to show them something very strange. Force the top card onto your spectator. You can use any force that you like. However, my preferred method is the "Criss-Cross Force" (page 7).

Turn your back and tell your spectator to look at their card and then write it down on the piece of paper.

2 Make sure they fold up this paper (so that you cannot see it). Now turn back around and burn the paper in the ashtray.

3 Tell your spectator that the ashes left in the tray are going to reveal what their card was. Your spectator will look slightly confused so cup some of the ashes in your hand and pat them onto your wrist.

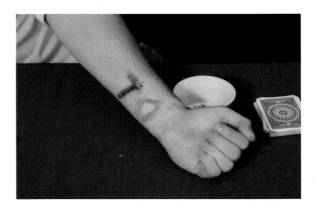

4 The ashes will stick to the parts of your arm that contain lip balm magically revealing the spectator's chosen card.

TORN AND RESTORED NAPKIN

EFFECT:

The magician visually tears and restores a napkin in front of their spectator.

PREPARATION:

A You will need two identical paper napkins or pieces of paper. Disposable napkins from restaurants work really well for this!

B Crumple one napkin into a tiny ball and place it in the palm of your right hand to conceal it from your spectators. Leave the other napkin on the table and you are ready to begin.

PERFORMANCE:

1 Let the spectators inspect the napkin on the table. Once they are happy that it is completely normal, pick it up with both hands. Make sure the knuckles on your right hand are facing the spectator, so they don't see the hidden napkin.

PRO TIP:

This is a great trick to do in a restaurant because they always have napkins lying around. Just make sure that your audience is sitting in front of you so that they don't see the hidden paper ball.

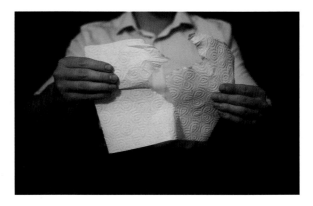

Now comes the only "hard" part of the trick. You need to roll the paper ball behind the napkin with your thumb as shown below. When practicing this trick, isolate this move and practice doing it over and over again until you build up the muscle memory to perfect it.

3 Tear the napkin down its center into two separate pieces. Continue tearing as many times as you like, keeping the paper ball behind the pieces.

You should now be in a position where you have one complete ball of paper as well as lots of little bits of paper, too. Fold the pieces of paper that you just tore up forwards into their own little ball as shown below.

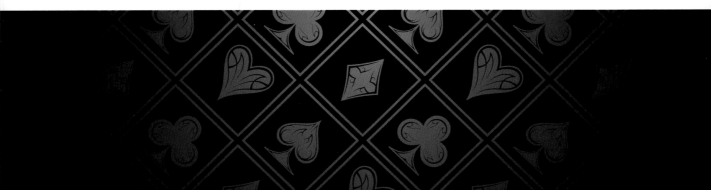

5 This will create two separate paper balls in your hand— one complete and one with torn up paper. However, from the spectator's point of view, it will look as if you have just one single paper ball in your hand.

6 Hold your right hand out flat so that your palm is facing upwards, and then rotate both balls so that the complete paper ball is on top. Then close your hand completely.

7 Snap your fingers and then pull out the complete paper napkin while keeping the torn ball concealed in your hand. This will create the powerful illusion that you have just restored the torn-up pieces of paper.

From here you can hand out the restored napkin to be inspected and pocket the torn pieces.

LINKING RUBBER BANDS

EFFECT:

The magician rubs two rubber bands together and they impossibly link.
He then unlinks them and hands the rubber bands out to be inspected.

PREPARATION:

For this trick you will need two rubber bands that are different colors. Stretch the rubber bands around your index fingers and ring fingers as shown.

B Now insert both of your thumbs into the top band.

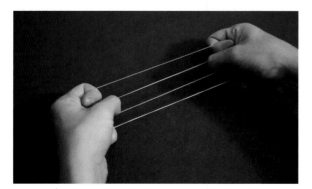

Use both thumbs to move the bottom strand of the top rubber band *under* the top strand of the bottom rubber band. Take a look at the picture for a visual reference.

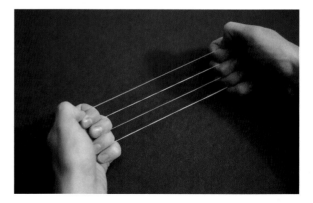

D Replace your thumbs with your middle fingers as shown.

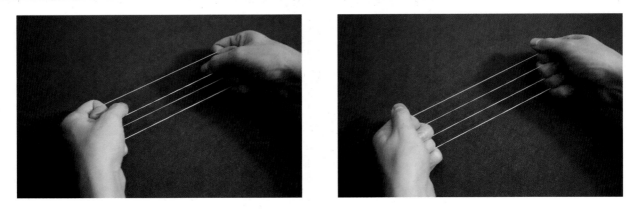

E Repeat exactly the same move as before. Use your thumbs to push the second strand (which is actually the bottom rubber band) below the third strand (which is the top rubber band).

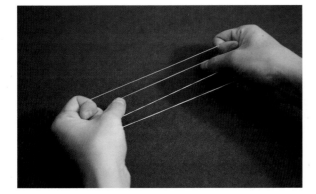

F As you did beforehand, replace your thumbs with your middle fingers. If you move your hands into fists, from the front it will look as if you just have two rubber bands in your hand. The spectator will have no idea that they are twisted around each other.

PERFORMANCE:

1 Fortunately, the next part of the magic trick is pretty much self-working. Display the rubber bands to your spectator.

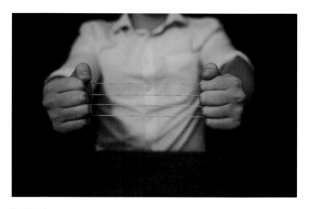

2 Then slowly release one of the middle fingers and carefully "catch" the bands with both your middle finger and corresponding thumb. Then rub both fingers together and let go, revealing the first link.

3 Repeat the same process but his time with your other middle finger. The bands will now "unlink." Everything can be inspected.

PRO TIP:

The preparation aspect of this trick only takes a few seconds to get into once you're well-practiced at it. However, you will want to hide the fact that you are setting up the rubber bands by talking to the spectator and distracting them from your hands. A really good way to momentarily distract them is to look into their eyes, say their name, and ask a question. This will give you the few seconds needed to prepare the rubber bands.

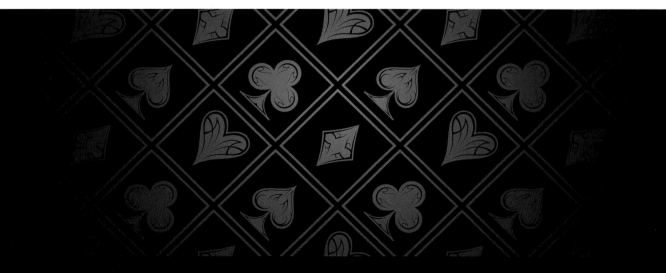

WHICH HAND?

EFFECT:

The magician correctly guesses what hand the spectator is hiding the coin in. This trick works nearly 100 percent of the time and will make you look like a master of body reading!

PREPARATION:

For this effect you'll need a coin. However, you could also use any small object such as a rubber band, sweet, etc. I often ask the spectator to empty out their pockets and then choose an object themselves.

PRO TIP:

This is a great little effect to do at a party or social event because it can be done completely surrounded. I usually like to repeat it two or three times to prove that it wasn't "luck" that allowed me to guess which hand the coin was in.

PERFORMANCE:

1 Give the coin to the spectator. Turn your back to them and tell them to put the coin in either one of their hands.

2 Now tell them to hold the hand with the coin in it above their head for fifteen seconds and say the magic word "abracadabra" three times slowly.

3 Once they have done this, instruct your spectator to hold both hands out in front of them in closed fists. Now turn around and say you are going to guess what hand contains the coin.

Look carefully at their hands and you'll notice that one hand will be paler than the other because the blood rushed out of it when it was above their head. In our example it is the spectator's right hand that is paler. As such, you know that this hand contains the coin.

From here, the rest of the trick is just showmanship. Slowly wave your hand over their closed fists and pretend to "sense" what coin the hand is in. Then point at the hand with the coin in it.

RESTORE SODA CAN

The magician shows a crushed, opened, and empty soda can. He then shakes the can and it visually "un-crushes" and reseals itself. He then opens the can and pours out the drink! Everything can be examined. This is easily one of the greatest tricks ever created.

PREPARATION:

This trick requires just one fizzy drink can. Yep . . . that's right! You don't need to switch the can out for another one; everything is self-contained. However, you need to set up the can in the following manner:

A Take a normal can of fizzy soda and place it on its side. Make a small hole in the side of the can about half an inch from the top (the top being where you drink from). This hole needs to be really tiny, so get a needle and prick the side of the can. Try and make the insertion somewhere that isn't too obvious. For example, if there is a pattern on the can, then make the hole there so it won't be noticed.

B When you pierce the can, the drink will squirt out. Keep letting the can expel the drink until there is around two-thirds left.

C Your next task is to crush the can. This is really easy—just squeeze it so that it is obviously dented and out of shape. Don't overdo the crushing and completely flatten the can.

D Next, take a small piece of paper and shade it in with a black pen. Cut it into an oval shape that is a similar size to the opening of the can.

E Now using saliva, just stick this to the top of the can where the opening would be if it were open. Your can should now appear crushed and empty.

PERFORMANCE:

Pick up the can and show your spectators that it is empty and crushed. Now grip the can in such a way that your thumb covers the little hole you made earlier. Begin to gently shake the can and the carbon dioxide within will begin to expand and reshape the can to its original condition.

Now that the can is restored, spin it around to show all sides to the spectator. As you do this, simply use your index finger to slide off and palm the black paper on top of the can.
You can now reveal that the can has been resealed!

1, 2, 3 The can will appear to uncrush itself as shown above.

PRO TIP:

The best way to present this trick is to do it seemingly spontaneously. So, set up the can in advance and then leave it somewhere that looks natural. For example, you could leave it in a fridge at a party, and then when someone asks to see a trick, open the fridge and restore the can.

4 Finally, open up the can and tip out the drink to show everyone that it actually contains the drink too!

NEEDLE THROUGH BALLOON

EFFECT:

The magician slowly pushes a needle through a balloon. Surprisingly, the balloon does not burst. Once the needle has been removed, you can then push it back through the balloon and make it burst whenever you like.

PREPARATION:

This is a simple optical illusion that only takes a few seconds of preparation. You will need a balloon, needle, and sticky tape. Blow up the balloon and then cut a tiny square of Scotch Tape from its roll.

A Stick the Scotch Tape to the balloon on the opposite side to the knot. Due to its transparency, this will be almost impossible to see.

PERFORMANCE:

1 Hold the balloon at your fingertips and show that it is completely normal. Then pass the needle around for examination. Once your audience is satisfied, slowly pass the needle through the Scotch Tape on the balloon. The tape will prevent the balloon from bursting.

Once you have demonstrated this, push the needle through an area of the balloon that does not contain any tape and it will burst.

PRO TIP:

When performing this trick, you need to come up with some good small talk to justify the fact that you are pushing a needle through a balloon. One of my favorite ways to present it is as an optical illusion. Tell your spectators that everything you see is not real. The needle is not really going through the balloon, instead it is all an illusion. Then give the needle to the spectator and let them try. Of course, the balloon will burst, proving your point!

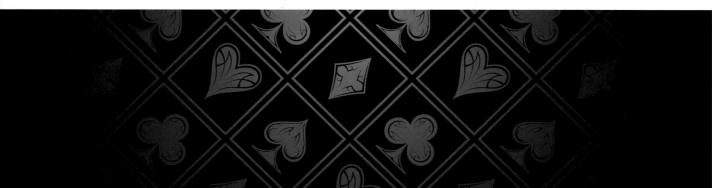

GUESS THE PASSWORD TO ANYONE'S PHONE

EFFECT:

The spectator gives the magician their phone. The magician guesses their PIN number and unlocks it.

PREPARATION:

This trick requires your spectator to have an iPhone.

PRO TIP:

The most important aspect of this trick is the justification for them to type in all of the numbers into their calculator. You want to stress the fact that the randomly generated number (which you could not have predicted) will magically let you know what their PIN code is.

PERFORMANCE:

Tell the spectator to open up their calculator app. Make sure they keep the phone close to their chest so that you cannot see it. Now tell them to enter a random four-digit number onto the calculator.

Instruct them to multiply that number by any two-digit number and press equals (=). Next, subtract any three-digit number and hit equals (=). Finally add their phone's PIN number and press equals. On their screen they should have a very large, and very random number. Tell them to read that number out loud.

Pretend to think about this random large number for a couple of seconds and then say that you have been able to deduce their exact PIN number from it. Tell them to press the "C" button to clear the calculator and then to give you the phone.

Once you have the phone, hold it so only you can see the screen and simply press the equals (=) button and the last number they typed (their PIN number) will appear. Now that you know their code, lock the phone and simply type in their password to unlock it. A true miracle!

RING UP RUBBER BAND

EFFECT:

A ring defies the laws of gravity and moves up a rubber band! This is a simple, visual, and devious magic trick that will leave your spectator frazzled.

This is a great little effect that can be done with borrowed items that you are likely to find lying around your house. I like to combine it with other illusions such as the French Drop vanish taught on page 46 and the "Linking Rubber Bands" taught on page 113. However, as a stand alone trick this is still very powerful.

This effect is also particularly good to perform on social media platforms (such as YouTube and Instagram) since it is easy to learn and looks incredibly visual.

PREPARATION:

A   I really enjoy performing tricks with devilishly simple secrets, and this is most certainly one of those. All you need for this trick is a rubber band and a ring. Both of these items can be borrowed. Break the rubber band in half and then thread it through the ring.

B   Hold the rubber band on either side of the ring using your thumbs and index fingers.

C   Pull the rubber band taut.

D Now lift up your left hand until the rubber band reaches a 45-degree angle. Let the ring slide down the band. Once you have practiced doing this enough, this setup will only take 3 seconds to get into.

PERFORMANCE:

1 Display the ring on the rubber band to your spectator. From their point of view, everything looks normal, but what they don't know is that you have stretched the rubber band in advance.

Slowly loosen your grip in your right hand. As you do this, the band will begin to contract, bringing the ring with it. This also creates the incredible illusion that the ring is defying the laws of gravity and can travel upwards. Once the ring has reached its final height, you can hand everything out to be examined.

The More You Look, the Less You See.

BETS

Fooling your friends is always fun, but why not add some sneaky bets into the mix too? Here are six of my favorite foolproof bets that you can take with you next time you are at a bar, a party, or someone's house.

FORK BALANCE

THE BET:

The magician bets the spectator that they cannot balance a fork, spoon, and a toothpick on the rim of a glass cup. The spectator will try to do this and inevitably fail. The magician then takes all three objects and successfully balances them! This bet works perfectly in restaurants where you will have easy access to all of these props.

PREPARATION:

All you need is a toothpick, a cup, a spoon, and a fork.

PERFORMANCE:

1 To begin, bend the middle two tines of the fork upwards slightly using your thumb. This will allow you to push the fork and spoon together. The middle two tines should be in the bowl of the spoon and the outer two tines need to be outside the bowl of the spoon as shown. This locks the spoon and fork together.

2 Now take the toothpick and push it through the middle tines of the fork.

3 The final step is to carefully place the toothpick on the edge of the glass cup. Make micro-adjustments by moving the toothpick forward and backwards to find the balance point. When you find the sweet spot, you can remove your hands, and everything will impossibly balance!

PRO TIP:

To take this effect even further, light a match and set the toothpick on fire at both ends. The toothpick will burn but amazingly the utensils will remain balanced!

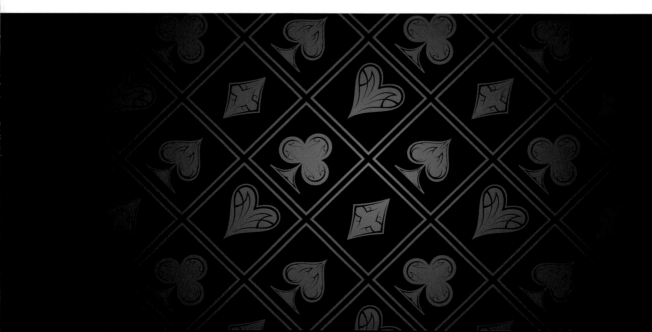

THE BOTTLE CAP BLOW

THE BET:

The magician takes a bottle cap and folds it in half. He then places the bottle on its side and puts the cap in the opening of the bottle.

He bets the spectator $20 that they cannot blow the bottle cap further into the bottle. It doesn't matter how many times the spectator tries; they will never be able to blow the cap into the bottle!

PREPARATION:

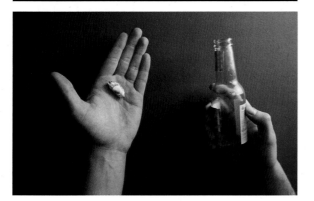

A All you need is a bottle that has a neck and a metal cap. Remove the cap and then fold it in half.

PRO TIP:

Make sure that the bottle cap is not too far in the neck of the bottle or sometimes it won't move when you blow! It is also a good idea to dry the cap on your shirt; the removal of moisture makes it easier for the cap to fly out.

PERFORMANCE:

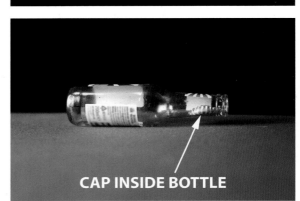

CAP INSIDE BOTTLE

BLOW ON THE CAP AND IT COMES OUT

1 The lovely thing about this effect is that it is completely self-working. As the spectator tries to blow the bottle cap, they are also blowing air into the bottle. This creates pressure within the bottle, expelling the cap *out* of the bottle, not into it. So, it is actually physically impossible for them to win this bet. As I'm sure you can imagine, your spectators will find this very frustrating, especially if there is money involved!

SODA CAN BALANCE

THE BET:

Bet your friend that you can balance a soda can at a 45-degree angle on the table. This is an easy bet that utilizes the laws of physics!

PRO TIP:

It is really important that you balance the can slowly. If you are too quick, the soda might spill everywhere!

   Also, it goes without saying that you should not carry out this bet near any electrical items, just in case someone knocks over the can.

PERFORMANCE:

1 Open up the can and pour out around one third of the drink. It is okay if you are a little off.

2 Now tilt the can to a 45-degree angle. You will notice the groove on the bottom of the can will naturally facilitate this movement.

3 Make micro-adjustments with your hands by pushing the can forward and backward until it balances. You are trying to find the equilibrium between the can and the liquid inside.

CRACK AN APPLE OPEN WITH YOUR BARE HANDS

THE BET:

The magician bets the spectator that he can crack an apple open with his bare hands. The spectator can inspect the apple and can even try to crack it open themselves. They take the magician up on the bet, and, as promised, the magician grabs the apple and splits it into two pieces using just his hands! If you have ever wanted to have supernatural strength, then this is the perfect trick for you.

PREPARATION:

A You will need an apple. The bigger, the better.

PERFORMANCE:

1 The amazing thing about this illusion is that there is no gimmick or advanced preparation. You are *really* going to crack the apple open with your hands. And don't worry—even if you are not very strong you will still be able to do this. It's about how you use your hand muscles; *not* how strong your hand muscles are. To begin, take a regular sized or large apple and remove the stem. Smaller apples will be much harder to break open.

Now place the fleshy part at the base of your thumb into the dip at the top of the apple.

PRO TIP:

This effect is actually easier to do than most people think. However, you need to develop the muscle memory in your hands to routinely perform it. So, grab a bag of larger apples and practice cracking them open!

Place the rest of your fingers around the bottom of the apple.

Two things are going to happen at once. Push your fingers upwards into the apple, while your thumbs push downwards. This will compress the apple. At the same time, use your wrists and thumbs to exert force outwards. This grip and movement will let you tear open the apple almost as if you were opening a book.

ONE HUNDRED WORDS

THE BET:

The magician challenges the spectator to say ten different words that do not use the letter "A." This of course is very difficult, but most spectators will manage it. Now challenge them to do twenty words. Naturally, this will be even tougher. While they are struggling, bet your spectator that you can do one hundred words! They are sure to take you up on the bet.

PREPARATION:

None.

PERFORMANCE:

The secret to this bet is devilishly simple. Just count from one to one hundred. You'll notice that none of these words actually contain the letter "A." One, two, three, four, five, six, seven, eight, nine, ten, eleven, twelve, thirteen, fourteen, fifteen, etc.

PRO TIP:

This is a great little "filler" gag that you can deploy whenever you need a quick break from performing. If you want to rest your hands for a couple of minutes before moving on to the next trick, give your audience this challenge. It will keep them entertained and also give you a well deserved rest!

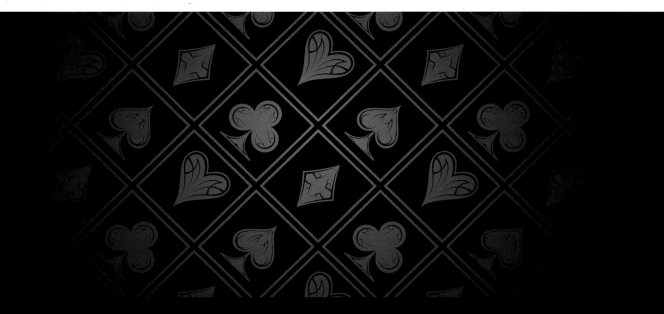

COIN BALANCE

THE BET:

You challenge your friend to balance a coin on the edge of a banknote. It doesn't matter how hard they try; they will always fail.

PREPARATION:

You will need a coin and a banknote.

PRO TIP:

If you want to take this to the next level, try stacking four coins on top of each other and giving the balance a go. This is much harder to do, but with some practice, you'll be able to pull it off every time.

PERFORMANCE:

1 You'll be pleased to know that pulling off this stunt is actually really easy when you know how. Take a coin and a crisp banknote. Fold the note in half along its long edge as shown.

2 Then fold it in half along its short edge.

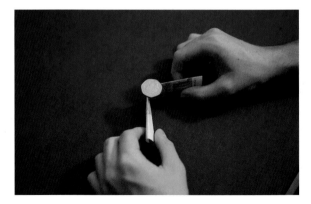

3 The note should now be in a V shape. Place the coin in the center of this V.

4 Take both ends of the note and carefully pull outwards. You'll notice that as the note straightens out, the coin will impossibly balance on its edge.

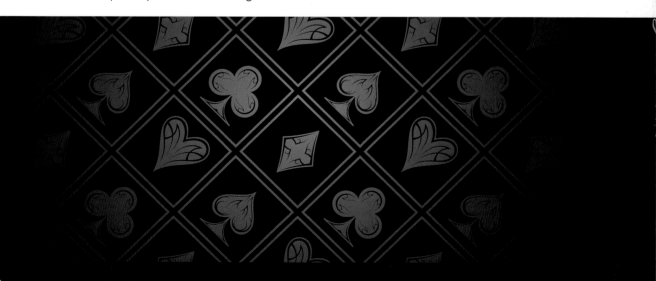

PRESENTATION TIPS

People often ask me "What makes the difference between a good magic trick and an astonishing one?" My answer is simple. How well the magician *presents* that trick. A good presentation will cause your spectators to clap their hands and say, "Well done," while an amazing presentation will make your spectators lose their minds and talk about *that* trick you did for weeks or months to come. As such, learning the secrets behind the effects in this book is a great start, but to really elevate your magic to that next level you need to spend time working on how you perform the trick.

So then, what makes an amazing presentation? Below I have outlined the seven most important things you need to keep in mind.

Practice = Confidence
An amazing presentation is one where the magician is confident, knows exactly what they are doing, and carries out sleights with conviction. The easiest way to become more confident is to practice. The old idiom "proper preparation prevents poor performance" rings true here. Take the time to sit down with your cards in front of the mirror and keep going over the trick until you have mastered it. Once the trick becomes second nature, you will be far more confident when performing it to others.

Use Your Family and Friends
This really helped me when I first started out in magic. Every time you learn a new trick, test it out on friends and family members first. This should be a low-pressure performance where you can receive friendly feedback on the trick and ways in which you can improve.

Think Positively
Although it sounds basic, being in the right mindset is one of the easiest ways to improve your performance. If you start the trick by thinking, "Oh gosh, they might figure me out," you'll come across as far less confident. Therefore, begin your tricks by focusing on what could go right, not what could go wrong. Think about the smile (or shock) on their face as you pull off that sleight you've been working on for the last few days. Repeat positive affirmations such as, "These spectators are going to have their minds blown when I show them this trick!" Doing so will naturally boost your confidence.

Make Eye Contact and Remember Names
One of the golden rules of magic is remembering the spectator's name. It helps to build a positive rapport and will make them far more engaged with, and involved in, your performance. Similarly, make an active effort to look them in the eyes when talking. This will help you come across as friendly, approachable, and inclusive.

Speak Clearly

Speaking clearly is a vital skill that will add clarity and confidence to your overall performance. You want to avoid speaking really quickly or very quietly. The best way to assess your speech is by recording your voice during a practice performance and then listening back to it with a critical ear. Think about the tone, volume, and pace of your voice and then note down any improvements you could make.

Wear Something You Feel Comfortable In

Long gone are the days where magicians had to wear top hats and three-piece suits. Nowadays, magicians can wear pretty much anything they like so long as they feel comfortable in it. That being said, make sure your clothes are presentable and practical. Have enough pocket space for you to carry all of your tricks in and make sure your clothes are clean and tidy to reassure the audience that they are in capable hands.

Add Comedic Value

Adding a comedic element to your performance always enhances the magic trick. Humor will come naturally from the trick you are performing since people are usually in a mindset where they want to have fun. However, there are plenty of one-liners and witticisms that you can learn and then interlace into your performance. Check out the "Joke Bank" on page 139 and work some of them into your patter.

Presentation Summary

Ultimately, you need to remember that there are two parts to any magic trick. Part one is perfecting the moves that enable the effect to work in the first place. Part two is mastering how you present and perform the trick. The second part, which we have just focused on here, requires time, thought, and practice. However, working on your performance always pays off and will help you transform an effect that spectators think is "cool" into a true miracle that will leave them scratching their heads when they try and go to sleep that night.

JOKE BANK

This is a collection of fun, quick-witted jokes that you can implement into your magic routine to make it more entertaining. Any experienced magician will tell you that you need to weave one-liners into your routine naturally. So read these jokes, find the ones that align with your performance style, and then add them to your patter!

Introducing a trick:

- "Ah darn, I've come to this show ill-equipped and underprepared. I wasn't aware I was doing it until around five weeks ago."
- "Before we begin, let me tell you a little bit about my background." Then turn around and start describing what is behind you.
- "A little bit about me before we begin. I've performed in front of The Prince of Wales, The Crown and . . . some other well-known pubs too."

Choosing a spectator:

- "I need a talented, beautiful, and lovely assistant to help me." Look directly at a spectator. "Do you know one?" Or say "Okay, okay I'll just do it myself."
- [Magician points to a spectator and says] "Where are you from?" [The spectator gives a location, e.g. Paris] "Sorry?" [The spectator repeats what they said] "No, no, I heard what you said. I am just sorry."

Choosing a card:

- "Yes, this is a trick deck. All the cards on this side are the same [point at the card backs], but every card on this side is different [point at the card faces.]"
- "I want you to think of a card. Any card you like, but don't let me purSPADE [persuade] your decision or anyKING [anything] like that."
- "Please select any card with your hand. No, with your clean hand."
- "Would you like to change your mind? No? So, you are happy with the mind you have got?"
- "Choose any card that you like. No, stop, not that one!"
- Tell the spectator to think of a card. "Now there is no way that I could know what card you are just *thinking* of right?" The spectator will agree. "Yep, that's what I thought. I guess I'll have to do another trick then."
- Once they have chosen a card say, "It's okay if I see your card. I've seen this trick before."

- If your spectator takes a long time choosing a card say "Take as long as you like. I get paid by the hour!" Pause for a moment while everyone laughs and then follow it up with "Yep, $2 an hour"
- Let the spectator pick a card and then say, "Show it to all of your friends." When the spectator doesn't show you the card say, "Okay I see how it is—I guess we are not friends then."
- Stick one card very obviously out of the deck and say, "Pick a card, any card. There are fifty-two different cards, fifty-two different possibilities!" Then really obviously try and make your spectator pick the card that is sticking out. If they take the card say, "Well this is going to be easy!" If they refuse to pick it, just sigh and go: "Tough crowd."
- Begin by saying that bad magicians are those who tell you to "Pick a card, any card". Then proceed to spread out the cards and instruct the spectator to "Pick a card, any card".

Shuffling the cards:

- Give the cards to your spectator and then turn your back to them. Instruct them to shuffle up the cards. As soon as you hear the cards being shuffled quickly say, "However, it is very important that before you start shuffling . . ."
- If you know how to do a fancy shuffle, ask your spectator, "Do you know what this is called?" They will most likely respond, "No." Then say, "It's called showing off!"
- Glue a deck of cards together and then instruct your spectators to shuffle it.

Revealing their card:

- If you are doing a mentalism routine that involves trying to guess their card say, "Hmm, I'm sensing that your card is. . . cherry-colored. No? Well, you clearly don't know what a black cherry is then."
- If you correctly guess their card say, "Phew, I'm glad that worked!" Then turn to your spectator and loudly whisper, "Thank you for helping me out, I'll pay you later."

If your spectators don't react:

- If you get no reaction when you finish the trick say, "That's okay, when I first saw this trick I was just as stunned and amazed as you are that I forgot to clap, too."
- If only one spectator laughs, ask them to run around the room so that you can imagine everyone else is also laughing.

If you drop the cards accidentally:

- "Sorry, did anyone else feel that sudden gust of gravity?"
- Point at a card that is face up and say, "Was that your card?"
- If someone is filming you with their phone, point at the camera and say, "Don't worry, we can just edit this out afterwards."

If you reveal the wrong card:

- "Darn, looks like you chose the wrong card."
- "Ah . . . give me fifty-one more attempts."
- "No, this is your card. I just changed it into another one when you weren't looking."

- When you get the wrong card, call them a liar. This always makes the crowd laugh.
- "Well. . . looks like I've just wasted fifteen years of practice."

If they ask to see a trick again:

- "Sorry, once is a trick, twice is a lesson."
- "Do what again? Did I miss something? What happened?"
- "Sure thing! But make sure you choose exactly the same card."
- "And why is that? Did you miss something?"
- "Well, if you liked that one, then you'll *love* this one."
- "But I did it right the first time."
- "Again? But the charge in my card teleportation device has run out."
- "I really don't know how I did it the first time."
- "I can't. My [coins/cards/object] is too tired."

If they ask to shuffle:

- "Just let me finish the trick first, and then you can show everyone your dance."
- "Well, I don't go around asking to touch your things."
- "Of course! Just let me finish the trick first!"
- "Only if you promise to put all the cards back in order afterwards."

If they ask how it is done:

- Spectator: "Can you teach me that?" Magician: "Well, can you keep a secret?" Spectator: "Yes!" Magician: "So can I."
- "I wish I could tell you but unfortunately it is against the rules of my cult."
- "Very well, thank you."
- "With great skill and dexterity."
- "Oh, it's really easy—just look up how to do the one-handed reverse triple scissor-cut back palm production."
- "I cheat, lie, and deceive—that's how!"
- "I could tell you, but I'd have to kill you. . . ." Smile and wink as you say this.
- "I actually have no clue how. It just kinda happens sometimes."
- "Hundreds of hours of practice and no social life."
- "I did it with a [deck of cards/a coin/a ring]."
- "Oh, it's really easy. Just practice for twenty minutes a day . . . seven days a week . . . for twenty-five years."
- "I had to make a pact with the devil."

If they say that they knew how you did the trick:

- "Well, that makes one of us then."
- Hand them the deck and let them do it. This will usually make them panic!
- "Great! Can you take over then—I really do need a break."
- "What a coincidence—so do I!"

- "Darn. Next trick, please close your eyes."
- "Really? Well you are going to have to explain it to me then because I haven't a clue how it works."

- "I went to Hogwarts."
- "Both my parents were gamblers . . . so I picked up some tips from them!"
- "Well, back when I was in prison."

- "No, these are normal cards! You can get them from any magic shop."
- "I wish they were."
- Wink at them and say, "Only when I'm holding them!"

- "And now it is time for me to perform the trick that you have all been avidly waiting for! My last one."
- Take a blank bit of paper and write the word "No" on it. Then show the other side to your spectator and say, "Do you know what is written on this card?" They will say "No." Then turn the paper around and say "Correct!"
- When closing your act say, "Thanks so much, guys. I've had lots of fun and can truly say that of all my audiences that I've performed for over the last five years, you have been the most recent."
- If you borrow a large amount of money from the spectator (let's just say $50) keep changing the value to something smaller when speaking. Say something like, "So as you know, this gentleman kindly gave me $10 which I then . . . What? Fifty? Okay sure. Anyway, I then took his $20 bill and [continue with the trick]."
- If your spectator gives you a large bill, you can also say something like, "Thank you for lending this to me—it's been a long time since I've been able to perform the disappearing money trick."
- If your spectator is young (under the age of fifteen) ask them for their name and if they are married.
- Smile at your spectators and say "I really couldn't have asked for a better, more respectful audience. . . because that would be impolite."
- "Want to see half a trick?" Proceed to reach into the deck and say "Was this your card. . ."
- Ask for a $10 bill from a spectator. After a few moments ask, "Who gave me this?" The spectator will say that they did. Then go "Thanks" and put it in your pocket. Then look at the rest of the audience and say, "You all heard him say that he *gave* me this money, right?"

CONCLUSION

I hope you have had fun learning some of the best kept secrets in the magic community. Now that you are equipped with the appropriate knowledge and skills, all I can say is "Go out there and start performing!"

Magic is a truly universal language that can take anyone back to that giddy childlike state where they start to believe that anything is possible. If you respect the art and put in the time to master it, it will return the favor one hundred times over by turning you into a more interesting, respected, and well-rounded person. Whether you want to learn magic to transform a typical Friday with your mates into one full of wonder and surprise or wish to become a full-time magician who can amaze crowds of people, you need to remember that there are two parts to any trick. The first part is learning the mechanics behind how the effect actually works and the second part is perfecting the art of performance. My concluding advice is to focus on mastering both of these areas. Doing so will enable you to wield an immense power to entertain and mystify anyone you meet with nothing more than cards, coins, or everyday objects that can be found lying around the house.

If you are interested in expanding your knowledge beyond this book, then you'll be pleased to know that there is a wealth of excellent material out there that will help you further refine your magical abilities. Check out the "Recommendations" section on page 145 for my suggestions about where to go from here.

I hope you have enjoyed learning these tricks and I would love to hear about your experiences performing them. Please reach out to me on my YouTube channel (search Oscar Owen on YouTube) and let me know how you have been getting on.

Stay magical, my dear friends.

Oscar Owen

YouTube: https://www.youtube.com/oscarowen
Instagram: https://www.instagram.com/Oscar/

RECOMMENDATIONS

The material listed below is what I recommend you read if you are looking to further your magic skills. I have deliberately only included a few resources in an effort not to overwhelm you with options as there are literally thousands of books out there.

Card Tricks:

- *The Royal Road to Card Magic* by Frederick Braue and Jean Hugard
- *Card Magic Pro Online Course* by Oscar Owen (A shameless plug but it is my online card magic course, teaching you everything you need to know about card magic!)
- *The Expert at the Card Table* by S. W. Erdnase

Coin Tricks:

- *Modern Coin Magic* by Bobo
- *Coin Magic: The Complete Book of Coin Tricks* by Jean Hugard
- *Al Schneider on Coins* by Al Schneider

Mentalism

- *Thirteen Steps to Mentalism* by Tony Corinda
- *Fundamentals of Professional Mentalism* by Bob Cassidy
- *Tricks of the Mind* by Derren Brown

The More You Look, the Less You See.

ACKNOWLEDGMENTS

This book wouldn't have been possible without the vision, insight, and creative thinking from hundreds of other magicians who have dedicated their lives to advancing this wonderful art. For those of you who wish to know more about where some of the tricks in this book originated, please follow the credits listed below.

- Criss-Cross Force—Max Holden (1925)
- Slip Cut Force—Discussed by Professor Hoffmann in *Modern Magic* (1876)
- Hindu Force—Theodore Annemann in *The Jinx 51-100, Issue 56* (1939)
- Bluff Control—Creator unknown, ideas first discussed in *Greater Magic* (1938)
- The Cut Control—Multiple sources of independent creation but Edward Marlo was a very influential figure on this move in *Control Systems* (1952)
- The Lazy Man's Card Trick—Published by Harry Lorayne in *Close-Up Card Magic* (1962), concept originally by Prof. Jack Miller
- A Crazy Self-Working Prediction—Principle, often referred to as "Miraskill" developed by Stewart James (1935)
- Do As I Do—Multiple sources of independent creation but the idea that two matching cards are selected first came from Friedrich W. Conradi-Horster
- Card In Orange—Concept of an object in fruit recorded by Professor Bellonie in *Die Zauberwelt* (1897)
- The Trick That Fooled Albert Einstein—Trick uses the principle of "Jackpot Coins" by Al Koran, however in this book I have used cards instead of coins.
- The French Drop Vanish—Popularized by Professor Hoffmann in *Modern Magic* (1876)
- The Instant Coin Vanish - By David Williamson in *Striking Magic* (1984)
- Coin Matrix—Based on the "Chink-a-chink" effect made popular in Edwin Sach's book *Sleight of Hand* (1877)
- JW Grip Production—Published by Horace Bennett in *Bennett's Fourth Book* (1981) but is credited Jimmy Wilson (hence the name JW Grip).
- The Mind Reading Test—Control Your Spectators Decisions—A classic effect that relies on the "multiple outs" principle
- Become A Mathematical Genius—See the "Magic Square" mathematical field for more information
- The Circle Routine—Taught by Vinh Giang on *52Kards YouTube Channel* (2017)
- Know What Word Your Spectator Is Thinking Of—Theodore Annemann popularized the center tear in *Mental Bargain Effects* (1935)
- Imagination Dice—Diamond Jim Tyler in *Bamboozlers* (2008)

ACKNOWLEDGMENTS

- "How to practice" quote—Wilfrid Jonson in *Magic Tricks and Card Tricks* (1950)
- Joke Bank—These gags come from all over the place. Many of them are my own, others I've read in books, heard other magicians say them, or have seen them online.

I also wanted to thank a few friends and family who have been by my side since the beginning of my own magical journey. Firstly, a huge thank you to my parents for getting me a video camera. Without your generosity, I wouldn't have been able to start putting up tutorials on YouTube and be where I am today. Also, a special thanks to my dad, Huw, who strongly "encouraged" me to perform magic to a waiter in a restaurant when I was thirteen. This was my first ever performance to a stranger, and despite being terrified, caused me to fall in love with magic after I successfully pulled off the trick. I also want to extend my gratitude to my mum, Rosie, who used to buy magic tricks for me and a wonderful fellow magician named Alisdair back when we were both ten. Your kindness has shaped who I am today, and for that, I cannot thank you enough.